A SITE ON THE UNESCO WORLD HERITAGE LIST

GUIDEBOOK

Enlarged and revised - 2013

TROİA/WİLUSA

GENERAL BACKGROUND AND A GUIDED TOUR
(INCLUDING THE INFORMATION PANELS AT THE SITE)
PREPARED BY THE DIRECTOR OF THE EXCAVATIONS

TROİA
Çanakkale-Tübingen TroiaVakfı

UNESCO

PATRIMONIO MUNDIAL • WORLD HERITAGE • PATRIMOINE MONDIAL

TROİA/WİLUSA

GENERAL BACKGROUND AND A GUIDED TOUR

INCLUDING THE INFORMATION PANELS AT THE SITE

PREPARED BY THE DIRECTOR OF THE EXCAVATIONS

Prof. Dr. Dr. h.c. Manfred O. Korfmann
Prof. Dr. Dietrich P. Mannsperger

English translation by
Jean D. Carpenter Efe

2013

Çanakkale-Tübingen Troia Vakfı (Foundation)

Publication Series: 1

Enlarged and revised 2013

ISBN 975-605-63925-0-4

To avoid religious bias, the neutral expressions BCE and CE,
"Before the Common Era" and "Common Era" replace BC and AD respectively

All proceeds from the sale of this volume directly benefit
the TROİA FOUNDATION and thus the site of Troia.

TROİA/WİLUSA
General Background and a Guided Tour, Including the Information Panels at the Site
Prepared by the Director of the Excavations

Prof. Dr. Dr. h.c. Manfred O. Korfmann

(Pre- and Protohistoric Archaeology)
Director of the Troia Excavations
Institut für Ur- und Frühgeschichte und Archäologie des Mittelalters

Prof. Dr. Dietrich P. Mannsperger
(Ancient Greek Philology and Numismatics)
Member of the Troia Excavations
Institut für Klassische Archäologie

Eberhard-Karls-Universität Tübingen
Schloss Hohentübingen
D-72070 Tübingen

Editor: Dr. Gebhard Bieg
English translation by Jean D. Carpenter Efe

Photographs, drawings and plans: G. Bieg, P. Jablonka, M. Möck (all of Tübingen University),
J. Essich, E. Riorden and R. Bullard

Reconstruction drawings: Ch. Haußner

Troia: Ein historischer Überblick und Rundgang/Manfred O. Korfmann

Printed in Turkey by
Biltur Basım Yayın ve Hizmet A.Ş.
Yukarı Dudullu Organize Sanayi Bölgesi 1. Cadde No: 16 Ümraniye-İstanbul
Tel: +90 444 44 03 Faks: +90 (216) 365 99 07-08 www.bilnet.net.tr
Zertifikat Nr.: 15690

Production by
Zero Prod. Ltd.
Abdullah Sokak 17, 34433 Beyoğlu - İstanbul - Turkey
www.zerobooksonline.com

TABLE OF CONTENTS

Manfred O. Korfmann and Dietrich P. Mannsperger
Homer, The Iliad and Its Consequences 7

Manfred O. Korfmann
A Tour of Troia 31

THE ENTRANCE

1 - The Wind Brought Wealth to Troia 33

AREA OF THE PARKING FACILITIES

2 - The Historical National Park of Troia 34

3 - A Hearty Welcome to Troia! 34

NEARBY THE WOODEN HORSE

4 - The Trojan Logo 38

5 - The Trojan Horse, Homer, and the Iliad 39

THE AREA OF THE EXCAVATION HOUSE

6 - Why Does Troia Have So Many Superimposed Strata?.... 41

7 - The Pithos Garden 68

THE AREA DEDICATED TO OUR SPONSORS

8 - The Eternal Stone of Troia 71

WITHIN THE RUINS OF TROİA

9 - History of the Discovery and Excavation of Troia 72
10 - The East Wall – Troia VI 78
11 - The Northeast Bastion – Troia VI 80
12 - Flora and Fauna 83
13 - The Citadel Wall – Troia II/III 84
14 - The Temple of Athena – Troia VIII/IX 86
15 - Time for a Break! 88
16 - The Megaron – Troia II/III 89
17 - The Fortification Wall – Troia I 91
18 - The Residence (Manor House) – Troia II 93
19 - Schliemann's Trench – Troia I 96
20 - Troia: the Various Levels 98
21 - The Ramp – Troia II 99
22 - The Palatial Residence (VI M) – Troia VI 102
23 - The Sanctuary – Troia VI-IX 106
24 - The Lower City of (W)Ilios/Wilusa – Late Troia VI 110
25 - The Water Cave of Troia/Wilusa (KASKAL.KUR) – Troia II-IX 112
26 - The Odeion and Bouleuterion – Troia IX 115
27 - The South Gate – Troia VI 119
28 - The Lower City – Troia VI-IX 121
Select Bibliography 127
Further Resources 130
In Gratitude 131

HOMER
THE ILIAD AND ITS CONSEQUENCES

Manfred O. Korfmann and Dietrich P. Mannsperger
Tübingen University

The wooden horse at Troia today.

Homer and the Iliad

It is to Homer that we owe much of the ethereal spirit of antiquity; without this bard we would never have met Hector or Achilles. It was Homer (Figs. 1-3) who –somewhere around 700 BCE– immortalized in speech first the ***Iliad*** and then the ***Odyssey***. This poet is one of the most miraculous the human race has seen, creating works whose monumental texts rival even the world's religious scriptures. Homer's epics represent the earliest surviving literature of Western civilization. Thanks to the verses of the ***Iliad*** and the ***Odyssey***, the myth of the Trojan War and the fate of those involved remains alive even today. That among all the early oral epics of the Greeks these in particular have survived is beyond all doubt a credit to their quality.

Homer's account of the "Trojan War" is much more intricate than a simple chronological narrative of events, one following upon the other (as is true of works by other early poets as well), an indication that the audience knew

Fig. 1
The blind Homer. Marble bust in Boston, after an original of the second century BCE.

Fig. 2 Homer enthroned, holding a scroll. Copper coin from Colophon (2nd cent. BCE).

Fig. 3 Homer as a seer. Silver coin from Ios, (4th cent. BCE).

Fig. 4 Graffiti from Homer's time on a geometric vessel from the Kerameikos cemetery in Athens (730-720 BCE).

the stories well. Homer's accomplishment lay in lifting specific events out of the greater context and arranging the plot anew –from the vantage point of these specific incidents. The result is a literary masterpiece, an epic poem in which even logic and history must sometimes bow to art. The narrative action is confined to a very brief period: a few days within the tenth and final year of the war. The theme is a schism in the personal relationship between the two most heroic leaders of the besieging troops, Achilles and Agamemnon, and the resulting consequences. Nevertheless, through flashbacks and glimpses into the future, the ***Iliad*** and the ***Odyssey*** present the entire story of what happened inside and outside the walls of Troia –or (W)Ilios, as the city was also known– the events from Paris' choice and the abduction of Helen (Fig. 5) to the victory over the city through the ruse of the wooden horse (Fig. 15). Soon after the composition of the epics, the theme was on the lips of all and ubiquitously represented in picture by a great variety of artists.

The influence of the myth upon Western culture has survived to the present day; consider, for example, Jean Giraudoux's *La Guerre de Troie n'aura pas lieu* and Christa Wolf's *Kassandra.*

Of Gods and Men

The plot of the *Iliad* is developed on two levels. From Olympus –shrouded in clouds– and from the high range of Mount Ida the gods look down on the inhabitants of Troia and the schemes of mankind. The deities not only take human form, but also often –only too often– share human

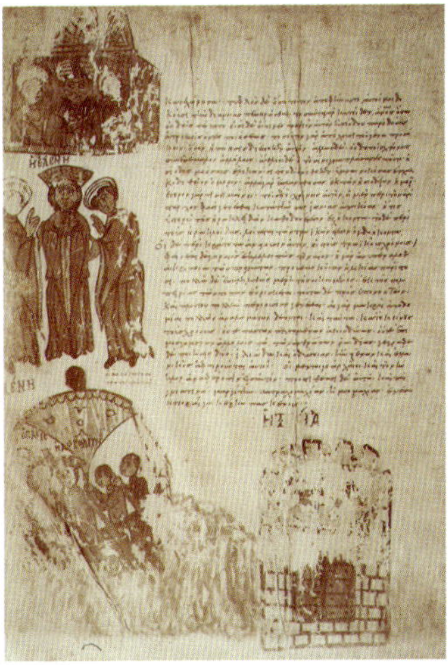

Fig. 5 Illustrated manuscript of the Iliad (10th cent. CE, now in Venice) showing Helen in Sparta and the arrival of Helen and Paris at Troia accompanied by Aphrodite. Introductory page.

Fig. 6 Opening lines of the Iliad with numerous scholarly comments, some as early as the third century BCE. From the same manuscript as Figure 5; taken from Constantinople to Italy in 1423.

Fig. 7 Apollo and Poseidon helping to construct the walls of Troia. Bronze coin of Ilion (2nd cent. CE).

Fig. 8 Head of Achilles on a silver coin of King Pyrrhus of Epirus (297-272 BCE).

Fig. 9 The goddess Thetis on a sea-horse, delivering weapons of Hephaestus to her son Achilles. Reverse of the coin in Figure 8.

impulses and emotions: pride and jealousy, love and hate, spite and pity. In the siege of Troia they take sides, not always without reason. The goddesses Hera and Athena feel rebuked by Paris (son of the Trojan King Priam), who –favoring the allure of Aphrodite who has promised him the most beautiful woman in the world as his wife– choses the latter over them. The promised beauty is none other than Helen, a daughter of Zeus already married to the Spartan King Menelaus. With Aphrodite's help, however, Paris manages to carry Helen off to Troia, thus unleashing the Trojan war by incurring the wrath not only of Menelaus, but that of all the Greek nobility who pledged their honor and protection at her wedding (Figs. 5-6).

The goddess Athena nevertheless proves fickle in her role, for from the very founding of the city, she has

Fig. 10
Achilles with his lance. Amphora attributed to the Achilles Painter (ca. 450 BCE).

Fig. 11 The Locrian Ajax in battle. Silver coin of Opos (ca. 350 BCE).

Fig. 12 Hector struggling with Ajax and Menelaus for the fallen Patroclus. Bronze coin of Ilion (217 CE).

served as the protectress of Troia; it is her temple that crowns the acropolis and her cult statue, the Palladion, that guarantees the might of Trojan rule. Indeed, well into historical times, it was her image –depicted in a most astounding range of styles– that was struck upon the official coinage of Ilion. Myth, however, demonstrates how

Fig. 13 Menelaus and Hector fight over the fallen Euphorbus. Cnidian plate (ca. 630/610 BCE).

fickle the deities may be; towards the end of the struggle, Athena allows Odysseus and Diomedes to sack the Palladion. She thus casts the dice in favor of the Achaeans, sealing the unfortunate fate of Troia.

Nor does the god Poseidon remain merciful to Troia. When the Trojan fortifications were first erected, both he and Apollo had come to assist, and in gratitude Laomedon (the Trojan ruler at the time) promised them the herd of immortal horses that Zeus had bestowed upon his grandfather. With Poseidon's help, the sturdy fortifications of Troia stood high and fast within a year (Fig. 7), during which Apollo had been herding the animals. Once the work was accomplished, however, Laomedon felt inclined to ignore his promise and chased the gods away. In consequence, Poseidon too joined the ranks of the gods and disappointed goddesses favoring the besieging Achaeans.

Fig. 14 Priam entreats Achilles for the body of Hector. Attic hydria (ca. 510 BCE).

Fig. 15 The Trojan horse. Corinthian aryballos from Cerveteri (ca. 560 BCE).

On the side of the Trojans remained Aphrodite –quite understandably– and others as well –including Apollo. During their many raids over the ten-year siege, the Achaeans had abducted Chryseis, daughter of a priest of Apollo, and thus encountered the wrath of the god, who in return infested their camp with a plague. To escape this punishment, the Greeks decide to return Chryseis, who has meanwhile been handed over as a gift to their highest in

Fig. 16 Aphrodite holding Eros, flanked by Menelaus and Helen. Attic crater (ca. 460 BCE).

command, Agamemnon. The general considers her return belittling to his person and demands in return the slave girl Briseis whom the Achaeans have earlier handed over to Achilles. Only after long strife is Briseis relinquished, thereby triggering the bitter wrath of Achilles that haunts the central theme of the *Iliad.*

Zeus sits alone on a neutral throne –generally on the peak of Mount Ida– from which he can direct the history of Troia and the fate of the heroes, often bridling the rebellious schemes of the other deities. Although from the very beginning the Trojan War was his idea, a plan to reduce overpopulation on the surface of the earth, it is only the wrath of Achilles that leads to his abstention from battle and the resulting loss of countless heroes.

Caught in the turmoil of the individual encounters, one may easily oversee the theme, interpreting the *Iliad* either as a poem of battle or of heroism. It is neither; the losses on either side are great, and the heroes generally represent tragic figures (Figs. 8-13). We understand them not only through their speech, but through their human character as well; it does not matter which side they represent. This becomes clearest in the closing lyrics of the ***Iliad*** where King Priam, son of Laomedon, at the end of the siege slinks by night into the presence of Achilles, the most dauntless warrior of the Achaeans, to beg for the corpse of his favorite son Hector, fallen at the hand of this warrior. His plea to recover the body of his son for a decent burial is finally granted by Achilles even though it was Hector who had killed his closest and dearest friend Patroclus in combat. Then the two of them, Achilles and Priam, weep together over the losses fate has brought them.

Homer concluded the ***Iliad*** with the burial of Hector although the war continued until Troia was vanquished (Figs. 15,16) –as we learn only from flashbacks in the ***Odyssey***. The impact of the ***Iliad***, in which Homer has depicted perhaps the most meaningless of all wars, however, lives on.

Myth and Politics

The fascination of myth is not restricted to poetics and the visual arts, for as the survival of the Trojan myth into modern times has demonstrated, what is "only art" can indeed alter the world. Responsible for this is perhaps not so much the oral poetic tradition of Homer's epic, but the lasting impressions of visual imagery. It is as

Fig. 17 Alexander the Great as son of Zeus Ammon. Silver coin of King Lysimachus of Thrace, minted at Lampsacus (ca. 290 BCE).

Fig. 18 Helios in a *quadriga* (four-horse chariot). Marble metope from the Temple of Athena at Ilion (3rd cent. BCE).

if the perspective of an all-seeing godhead granted Homer and his listeners/readers immediate visions of the scenes: Olympus, Athos, and Mount Ida; the isles of Samothrace, Imbros and Tenedos; the fortress of Troia with the Scaean Gate and the two springs below; the River Scamander; and the beached ships of the encamped Achaeans. The adroit actions and the characters as well are so full of life that they shine as brightly as personalities from the pages of documented history. Not only have refined aesthetes, but popular politicians and sharp-witted academicians as well been impressed by the potency of this literature. Politically significant remain the various analogies posited between the struggle over Troia and the East-West controversy –and that between Europe and Asia (or vice versa). Those in history afflicted by such challenges have often recalled the epic model. Under Persian rule in Anatolia the East was dominant; nevertheless, before crossing the straits at the Hellespont with his massive army in 480 BCE, the Persian King Xerxes stopped to pay a visit to

Fig. 19
Aeneas carrying the Palladium (symbol of Athena) in his right hand and his father Anchises on his back. Silver coin struck by Julius Caesar (ca. 47 BCE).

Fig. 20 Portrait of Julius Caesar on the obverse of a silver dinar (ca. 44 BCE).

Fig. 21
Caesar Octavianus Augustus. Silver coin (ca. 34 BCE).

the city of Priam, where he sacrificed a thousand head of cattle to the Athena of Ilion. The reverse occurred with the Asian invasion of Alexander the Great in 334 BCE; Alexander (Fig. 17) then offered sacrifices at the tomb of Achilles, where he bemoaned that he had no bard such as Homer to glorify his own deeds. In Alexander's honor his followers later rebuilt the downtrodden Ilion and erected a magnificent temple to Athena, only scattered remnants of which are visible today (Figs. 18, 80-84). It was then the turn of Antiochus I (281-261 BCE) to rout from the site the Galatians, Celts who had spilled into Asia Minor from Europe.

As early as the third century BCE, Rome began to acclaim its Trojan descent. The city goddess Roma

Fig. 22
Busts representing the goddess Roma and the Roman Senate flanking a statue of Athena Ilias. Bronze coin of the Emperor Caligula. 37 CE. From Ilion.

Fig. 23
The goddess Roma holding the Palladium. Gold coin of the Emperor Antoninus Pius (ca. 150 CE).

Fig. 24
Silver medallion portraying Constantine the Great with a monogram of Christ on his helmet and the Roman she-wolf on his shield (ca. 315 CE).

appeared on coinage as a Trojan, donning a Phrygian headdress. The same held true for the "Trojan" goddess Venus/Aphrodite. As mother of the renowned hero Aeneas –who led the surviving Trojans to Latium in Italy where they settled and established the lineage of the Roman population (Fig. 19) – she was therefore the patron goddess of Julius Caesar (Fig. 20), who dominated Roman politics from 60-44 BCE. Julius' patrician ancestry –that of the ***Iulii*** or Julians– harked back to Aeneas' son Ilos (Iulus or Julus Ascanius) and marked the family as potential rulers. Julius Caesar dreamed of an incursion against the Parthians, following once more upon the footsteps of Alexander the Great. Rumor had it that he wished to establish a new capital in the "old homeland" of Troia; any such plans, however, were thwarted by his assassination. Such a step would have been very plausible, for Troia lay most strategically on the boundary between the Occident and Orient –and between the Mediterranean and the Black Seas as well– a location as practical as it was symbolic.

Julius' heir and successor, Caesar Augustus (30 BCE-14 CE; Figs. 21, 116), felt a need for caution, however; the poet Horace had warned him that "only as long as the seas between Rome and Ilion continue to swell will Roman rule survive." (***Odes*** III 3, 37-38). Augustus nevertheless supported the mother-city as much as he could, as the coins struck here demonstrate. Images on coinage were by this time in antiquity a tried and true method of publicizing political might. On the coins struck under Caligula (37-41 CE) and the following Roman emperors as well, Troia and the Athena of Ilion received a fair share of official approbation (Figs. 22, 23).

It was first under Constantine the Great (306-337 CE; Fig. 24) that the tables turned. It was Constantine who first established the Eastern Roman Empire from what is now Istanbul on the Bosphorus, having first chosen Ilion as the location for his new capital. Construction here had already begun before his final option in 326 CE for Byzantion, which he then renamed Constantinople. Its environment was geographically more opportune: better provided with surrounding arable lands to feed the population of a growing capital. Although under Constantine Christianity was declared the official religion (as clearly seen from the monogram of Christ newly portrayed on his helmet), traditional cults persisted in Constantinople as well as in Ilion. When the later Emperor Julian (Julian the Apostate, 361-363 CE) visited Ilion in 355 CE, he found fires still burning on the pagan altars of the bishopric –and Hector's cult statue newly swabbed with sacred ointments! Throughout the Byzantine period we find mention of this bishopric; later municipal records dwindled away; only myth and legend survived.

Fig. 25 The citadel and lower city of Troia in the landscape of the thirteenth century BCE (Troia VI). Reconstruction from the SE, with the islands of Tenedos and Imbros (with the peak of Samothrace behind) on the horizon. © Ch. Haußner.

The Legend of Troia

The medieval romances of Troia, knights' tales dating from the 12th and 13th centuries (e.g. those of Benoît de Sainte-Maure, Konrad von Würzburg, and Herbort von Fritzlar) recount the alleged testimonies of two veterans –eye witnesses of the fall of Troia: the Cretan Dictys (variously assigned to the 1st-3rd centuries CE) and the Phrygian Dares (2nd-5th centuries CE). In consequence, Franks and Burgundians, Normans and Britons, and the Turks as well as the Romans began to see themselves as descendants of the Trojans. Particularly in the period following Charlemagne, the Franks benefited by cajoling the folk of their newly established empire with this legendary heritage, if only outwardly supported by false premises (that Xanten = Xanthos, and that Colonia Traiana could be read as Colonia Troiana).

The knights of the Fourth Crusade (1202-1204), which never reached Jerusalem but was instead directed against

Constantinople, partially justified their (truly) devious schemes with the excuse that they had come to avenge the siege of Troia. As the crusader Peter von Bracheux explained to an enemy commander, "Troia belonged to our ancestors, and those who managed to survive came to live here where we are from –and because they were our ancestors, we have come here to re-conquer this land of theirs."

Very similar was the attitude of Mehmet the Conqueror. After the fall of Constantinople, he too visited Troia and the burial mounds in the plain (ca. 1462) to make it clear to all that the disgrace against his lands had finally been avenged.

Troia, however, was much more than a focus serving to legitimize political actions. The story of the Trojan War became one of the foundation stones of the sphere of the Greek and Roman civilizations –the heart of culture in the ancient world. The high and late Middle Ages traced "chivalry" and "nobility" back to this supposedly common story. Thus the feats and deeds ascribed to the Trojan legend have embroiled Troia and its landscape in the very roots of western culture and history.

Myth and Scholarship

Homer presents quite an accurate description of the Trojan landscape ca. 700 BCE. The poet and his compatriots must have wandered across the plain of the Scamander, taking it all in with a keen perception, strolling as far as the former harbor –by then silted up– on the Aegean shore (Fig. 25). In the eighth century BCE, remnants of the acropolis walls would have projected above the still-visible fortifications of the lower Trojan settlement even though nothing more was to be seen of the beleaguered camp where the Achaean ships had been beached. This too is reflected in the epic: contemplating the strong fortifications of the Achaean camp, Poseidon complained that the Trojan walls he has built have been cast into shadow by the walls protecting the ships, whereupon Zeus suggested that the "Earth-Shaker" destroy the walls and cast them into the sea upon the retreat of the Achaeans.

Fig. 26 Ballıdağ near Pınarbaşı (an early candidate for the site of Ilion), a work of William Gell (Gell, *Topography of Troy*, pl. 35, London 1804).

Most classical philologists of the 19th and early 20th centuries interpreted the context of the epic as sheer fiction; they most painstakingly contested every detail. Upon occasion the scholars would go so far as to deny the existence of Homer. Nevertheless, travelers had been combing the region since the 17th and 18th centuries (a period of enlightenment) for traces of what they had learned in their youth from Homer's epics and still cherished. The Hellespont, the islands, the mountains and even the rivers they were able to identify, but they could find no seaside trace of any fortifications to mark the camp of the besiegers. Travelers here had naturally speculated where Priam's citadel might lie buried; during the 18th and 19th centuries most opted for a militarily strategic settlement site known as "Bounarbashi" (Pınarbaşı) or "Ilium Vetus" (Fig. 26) some eight kilometers south of the unassuming mound of Hisarlık. Although the latter rose only 31 m above the plain and covered an area no larger than that of a good-sized football stadium, it had long been assumed the site of Troia by various scholars in Greece and Rome. They believed Ilios lay here, and therefore the site was known as "Ilium Novum" or "Ilium Recens" in the 18th and 19th centuries. In 1863, then, the Englishman Frank Calvert finally set spade to earth, followed in 1870 by the German Heinrich Schliemann (who by that time also claimed Russian and American citizenship). Both explorers had been directed to the site by Homer.

The Archaeological Evidence

Curiously enough, however, nearly all the remains exposed by Heinrich Schliemann and Wilhelm Dörpfeld in the excavations of 1871-1894 represented an earlier unidentified prehistoric settlement; the same holds true for the American excavations of 1932-1938 directed by Carl W. Blegen. The bulk of the archaeological evidence, although of great scholarly interest, was centuries removed from the events of Homer's *Iliad*, generally accepted as

Fig. 27 The "Lion Crater", a vessel locally produced in Mycenaean style (A7.96 from Troia VI i).

Fig. 28 The 1999 excavations at Beşik-Sivritepe with Beşik-Yassıtepe (excavated 1982-87) in the background.

having taken place in the early 12th century BCE. Thus we recognize today that the various "Treasures of Troia" recovered by Schliemann had been deposited some 1250 years before the time of Priam. Even the impressive fortification walls of Troia VI discovered by Dörpfeld as early as 1893-1894 (Figs. 49, 51) –now conclusively dated through pottery to the Mycenaean period and thus enabling us to reconstruct what must have been the "Citadel of Priam"– long failed to impress many skeptics.

It was the Tübingen University excavations of 1982-1987 at the north of Beşik Bay some eight kilometers southwest of Troia on the Aegean coast (Fig. 28) that first confirmed the critical location of the Trojan harbor (Fig. 29). Here we discovered a cemetery of the 14th century BCE, as well as the archaic settlement of Achilleion (7th/6th cent. BCE); investigation of a nearby tumulus also confirmed its status as a Hellenistic monument most probably honoring the cult of Achilles. Although by no means contradictory to the content of the ***Iliad*** –or the ***Odyssey***– both of which reflect the environment of the late eighth century BCE, the principle evidence exposed here once more emphasized prehistoric settlement, most particularly the Neolithic period (5th millennium BCE) and the Early Bronze Age (3rd millennium BCE).

The new campaigns initiated at the site of Troia itself in 1988 are likewise archaeological in focus. At this most strategically located point lie both the anonymous prehistoric settlement and the historical site of Ilion that survived through Hellenistic and Roman times. Here lies information vital to both prehistory and classical archaeology. A possible "historical core" for the ***Iliad*** nevertheless –though relegated to the background– has not been lost from sight.

From the very earliest of these campaigns onward, the remains of most impressive streets and walls from Roman Ilion came to light; it was not long then before we discovered that a lower town had surrounded the acropolis of Troia/Ilios as early as the 13th/early 12th century BCE. Measurements taken in 2003 revealed that this covered an area of at least 300,000 m^2; thus Troia reached dimensions more than fifteen times as great as had ever been suspected. Historical sources tell us that the Greek city of Thebes (ca. 30 ha) was no larger, nor that of Pylos (ca. 20

Fig. 29 The Aegean realm, home of the Myceneans and Trojans (partially under control of the Hittites). Topography of the Ancient World Mapping Center, University of North Carolina, Chapel Hill. Particularly of note here is the potential of Troia as a bridge between Europe and Asia.

ha); nor could Mycenae (32 ha) have far surpassed it. Seen in this light, the city not only justifies the descriptions of Homer, but reaches a scale impressive enough to deserve its obviously important status with the Hittite Kingdom as Wilusa, annexed as a vassal state around 1285 BCE (during the period of Troia VII a or VI i).

Such evidence certainly seems to corroborate the existence of the large site recognized by the poet in the extensive remains still visible at the end of the eighth century and celebrated in his epics. What remains unconfirmed is a struggle over Troia as historic and heroic as that depicted in the ***Iliad***. Whether or not the powerful Achilles, mighty Agamemnon, crafty Odysseus and grief-stricken Priam played out their parts upon the landscape here must remain a mystery. What "proof," however, do we seek of them? The ***Iliad*** speaks for itself as an outstanding and international literary masterpiece that by no means demands any "confirmation" from archaeology.

A TOUR OF TROİA

Manfred O. Korfmann

THE ENTRANCE

As a respected visitor (or visitors), we heartily welcome you to this site, where your number will soon total a half a million per year, as predicted for 2013 –or perhaps even 2014! The site indeed deserves such interest. However, we wish to inform you that the entrance and parking fees are not used for excavation, academic research, or restoration (including paths and information panels), but are appropriated by the national authorities for other necessary expenditures.

The budget supporting the archaeologists participating in the recent excavations at Troia (1988 onward) is –quite typically– dependent upon scholastic resources (i.e., university contributions and those of academic institutions such as the Deutsche Forschungsgemeinschaft). Additional funds are provided by sponsors and individual donors, many of whom are interactive participants in the "Friends of Troia" program established in Germany, the US (through the Institute of Mediterranean Studies) and Turkey (here in Çanakkale). Long-term support or large bequests are best handled through the Troia Foundation (either the TROİA VAKFI here in Çanakkale or the TROİA STIFTUNG in Tübingen), which benefits from the sales of this guidebook as well. Should you wish to comment upon our efforts here at Troia –or perhaps wish to involve yourself in helping us intensify them, please do not hesitate to communicate with us at

http://www.uni-tuebingen.de/troia/
or by email: troia.projekt@uni-tuebingen.de

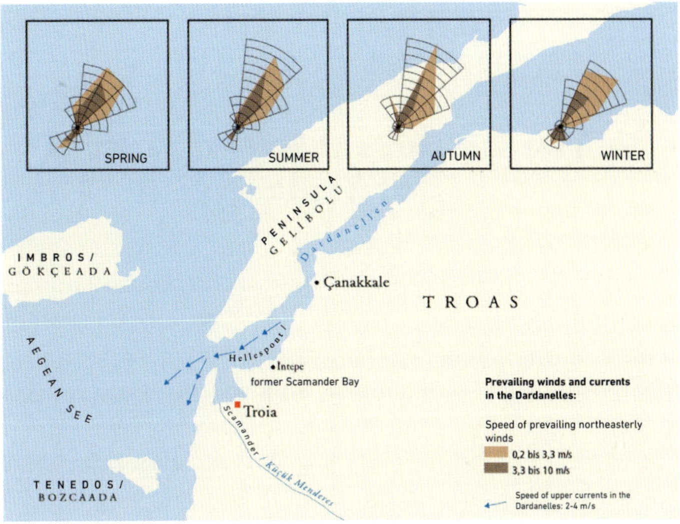

Fig. 30 Prevailing winds and currents in the Dardanelles.

1. (Info Panel) The Wind Brought Wealth To Troia

Geography in particular has proved a fantastic asset for Troia. The currents issuing from the Dardanelles and the prevailing northeastern winds very frequently forced ships bound for the Black Sea into the nearby harbor of Beşik Bay, where they had to bide their time waiting for the occasional southern breezes (Fig. 30); the technique of sailing against the wind was not mastered until the first century BCE.

AREA OF THE PARKING FACILITIES

2. The Historical National Park of Troia

On September 30, 1996, the Turkish government declared the site of Troia and the immediate surroundings a National Historical Park (Fig. 31). Within an area of some 136 km^2, the park includes an impressive number of archaeological sites dating from the Neolithic period through recent times (memorials to the many lives lost in the Battle of Gallipoli in 1915). No less important than the cultural heritage is the natural heritage, for modern agriculture is increasingly taking its toll. The last zones preserving an ecology relatively untouched by human progress are now under threat. A master plan for the park aims to protect both cultural and natural legacies. We must preserve the landscape of Homer so that coming generations can fully grasp the literary heritage through the message of the countryside.

3. (Info Panel) A Hearty Welcome to Troia!

Welcome to Troia, the legendary City of Priam! It was here, beginning in 1871, that the first chapter of modern archaeology was written. The tour of the site that is mapped out in this book (see the fold-out plan toward the back of the guide) will accompany you along a circular stroll through remains from the various phases.

An international excavation team under the direction of Professor Manfred Korfmann resumed archaeological campaigns here in 1988 after a long 50-year pause. During the summer months, Troia offers you a live "on-stage" view of archaeology in the works, an experience to be enjoyed at relatively few sites.

The Ministry of Culture and Tourism of the Republic of Turkey, the firms of Siemens Sanayi ve Ticaret A.Ş. and Mercedes-Benz Türk A.Ş., as well as generous patrons such as James H. Ottaway provide substantial ancillary support for the efforts of the dedicated men and women forming the archaeological and scientific core of the Tübingen University excavations. Only thus has it been possible to reveal more cultural background and throw some light upon certain riddles in the Trojan myth. It is thanks to the ideals and material contributions of many enlightened people that Troia (since 1998 included in UNESCO's "World Heritage" list of sites outstanding in the history of mankind) will be preserved for future generations as well. Hopefully you have set aside enough time to look carefully at what is here, read along, direct your thoughts into the past –and dream. The effort is well worth it here in this historical landscape celebrated worldwide.

Fig. 31 The Historical National Park of Troia.

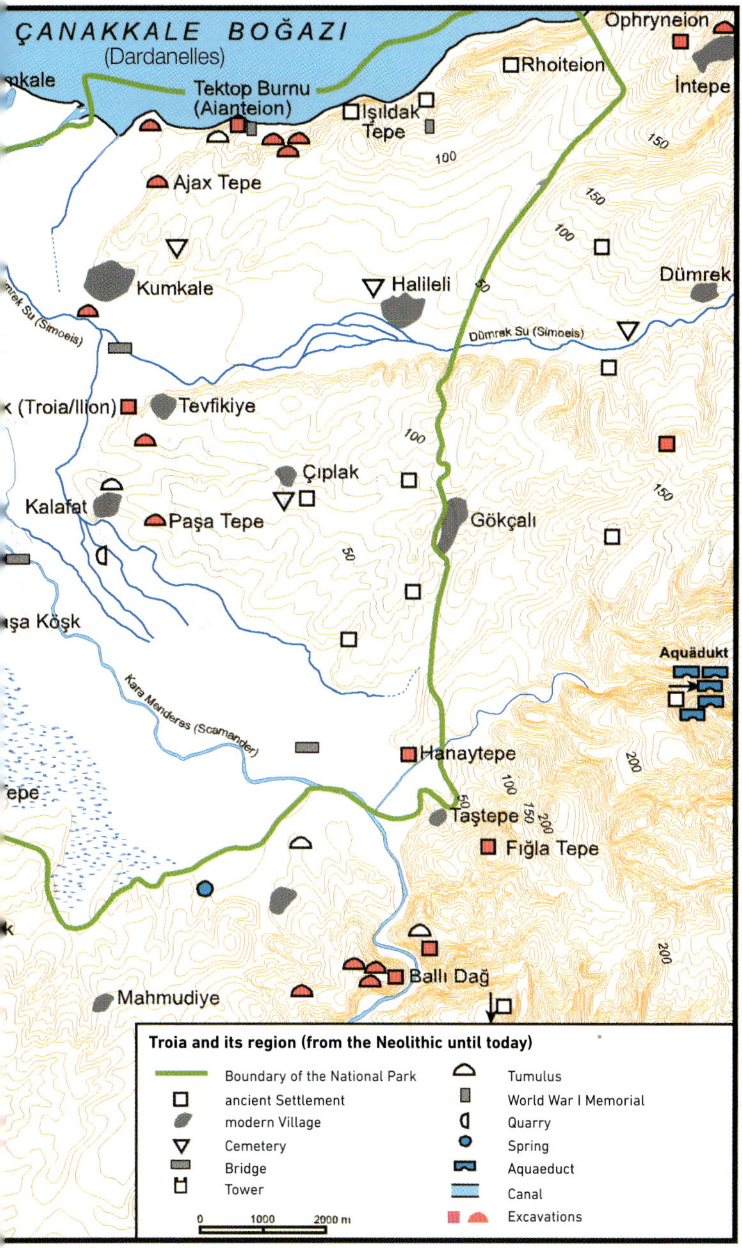
ÇANAKKALE BOĞAZI
(Dardanelles)
Tektop Burnu
(Aianteion)
Işıldak Tepe
Rhoiteion
Ophryneion
İntepe
Ajax Tepe
Kumkale
Halileli
Dümrek
Dümrek Su (Simoeis)
(Troia/Ilion)
Tevfikiye
Çıplak
Kalafat
Paşa Tepe
Gökçalı
Kara Menderes (Scamander)
Aquädukt
Hanaytepe
Taştepe
Fığla Tepe
Ballı Dağ
Mahmudiye
Troia and its region (from the Neolithic until today)
Boundary of the National Park
ancient Settlement
modern Village
Cemetery
Bridge
Tower
Tumulus
World War I Memorial
Quarry
Spring
Aqueduct
Canal
Excavations
0 1000 2000 m

NEARBY THE WOODEN HORSE

4. (Info Panel) The Trojan Logo

A biconvex Bronze-Age seal discovered in 1995 now represents the earliest securely dated evidence of writing at Troia (Fig. 32). It displays in an Anatolian hieroglyphic script commonly employed by the Hittites on seals as well as monumental inscriptions (the latter generally in Luwian). The Luwians were –like the Hittites and the Greeks– an Indo-European people. On one face (Side 1) we see the incomplete name of a scribe; on the other (Side 2), that of a woman, likewise incomplete. It comes from a stratified context, a house of Troia VII b 2 inhabited ca. 1130 BCE.

What is remarkable about this seal is the material; it is bronze, whereas most seals of this period were carved in stone.

Side 1 carries a man's name (three syllables, perhaps to be read as Tarhun-tà-nu); after first identifying him as a scribe, it wishes the bearer of the seal good luck.

Side 2 clearly bears the symbols for "good" and "woman."

Fig. 32 The bronze seal with Luwian script found in Troia VII b.

5. (Info Panel) The Trojan Horse, Homer, and the Iliad

Homer lived in the Ionian region of Asia Minor toward the end of the eighth century BCE and greatly enriched the literary heritage of antiquity. Were it not for this bard, we would know of neither Hector nor Achilles.

The epic poems of the Iliad and the Odyssey, ascribed throughout antiquity to Homer, represent stories that had been passed down in the oral tradition from the second millennium BCE. A few more centuries passed, however, before they were finally written down in verse (ca. 700 BCE). This suggests that Homer might have been the greatest poet who ever lived; both the aesthetic and historical impact of these epics rival even the religious scriptures of the world. These epics are the earliest surviving texts of western culture, and even today the Trojan War is a popular myth, with the fates of the heroes recounted in the lyrics still living on in our culture today.

The theme of the Iliad, although focused upon a single episode within the ten-year siege of Troia, nevertheless encompasses the whole of the myth. The climax of the Iliad is not the fall of Troia, but the deaths of the Trojan warrior Hector and the Greek Patroclus within the tenth and final year of the struggle. By selecting the duel of these two heroes from the legend and focusing upon the wrath of the Achaean Achilles, the poet has brought the theme of personal conflict and its consequences to the fore.

Epeidos finally builds the besieging Greeks a huge wooden "Trojan horse," in the belly of which the bravest of their heroes hide. Leaving the horse on the shore, the fleet apparently sails off into the sunset (but in fact drops anchor behind the nearby island of Tenedos). Despite a clear warning from Laocoön, the Trojans pull the wooden horse into the city as a tribute to their patron goddess Athena. During the night, then, the Greek heroes silently creep forth, light a beacon to call the ships back, and open the city gate to their comrades.

With this ruse, Troia is vanquished; after ten years of siege, the city has fallen. The saga of the city, however, does not end with Homer's epics; the story of the fugitive Trojan Aeneas' eventual founding of Rome is continued in the Aeneid of the Roman poet Virgil.

The wooden horse you see today (Fig. 33) is the 1975 creation of the Turkish artisan İzzet Senemoğlu.

Fig. 33 The wooden horse at Troia today.

THE AREA OF THE EXCAVATION HOUSE

6. (Info Panel 1a) Why Does Troia Have So Many Superimposed Strata?

The settlement mound of Hisarlık, directly on the Asian coast of the straits of the Dardanelles, gradually rose higher and higher. This is primarily due to two factors.

1. Strategically located, it was inhabited continuously for a period of some 3000 years.
2. Phase after phase, the residences were constructed primarily of sun-dried mud-bricks.

Although practically unknown in Europe, such bricks of tempered clay (similar to stucco) are characteristic of construction in the Near East. These brittle sun-dried bricks, however, offered no possibility of reuse; the earlier houses would be leveled and built over with structures of new mudbricks prepared of mud, temper and water near the foot of the mound; these too would eventually be destroyed and/or razed, thus contributing to a continuous "elevation" of the site.

Archaeological "digs" can thus (Figs 34-37) separate the more recent finds (above) from those preceding them (stratified below). The lowermost seven "parcels" –or periods– of the stratified settlement deposit at Hisarlık (Troia I-VII = Early Bronze Age-Early Iron Age) represent more than 50 renovations on the mound. Above these periods lie the Greek and Roman cities of Ilion and Ilium (Troia VIII and IX respectively), succeeded by the Byzantine epoch (Troia X). This artificial or manmade "hill" rises more than 15 meters.

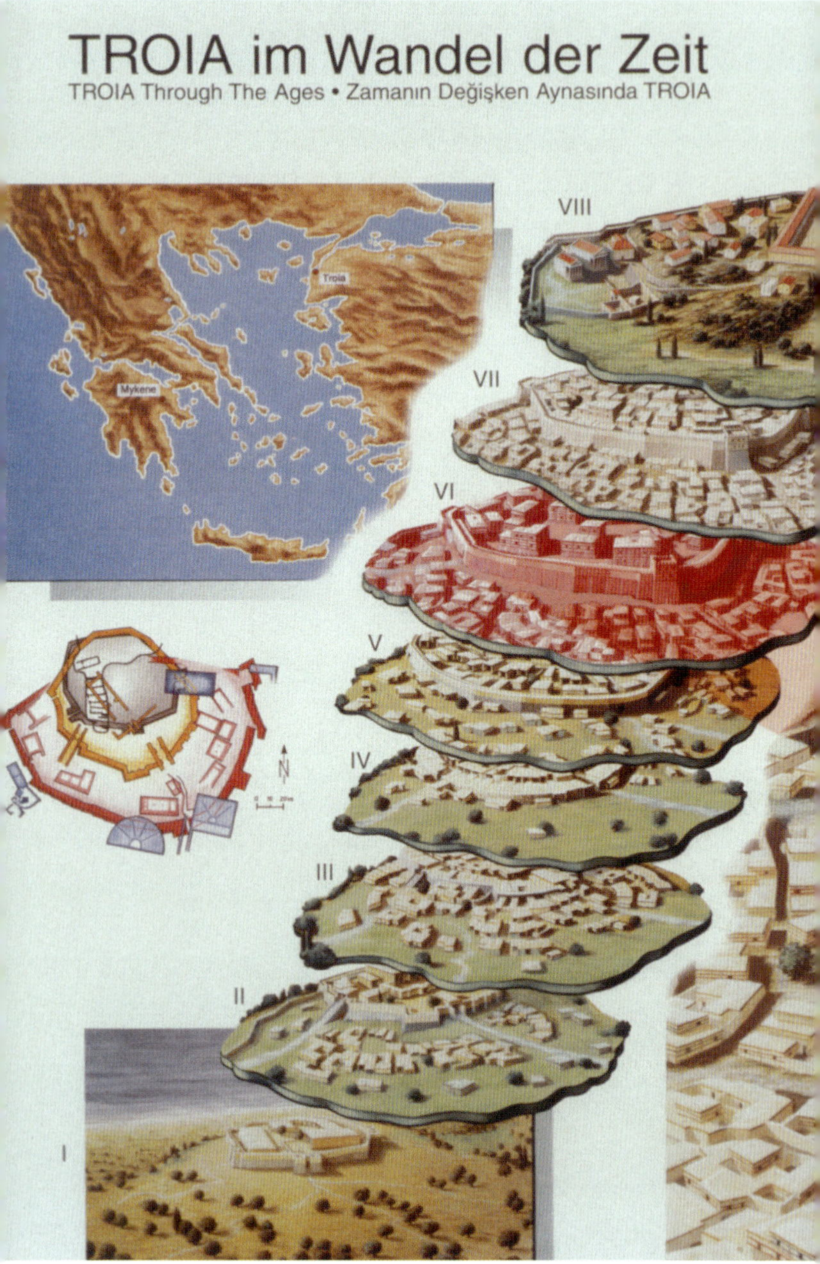

Fig. 34 Composite reconstruction of the site: periods I through IX (© Ch. Haußner).

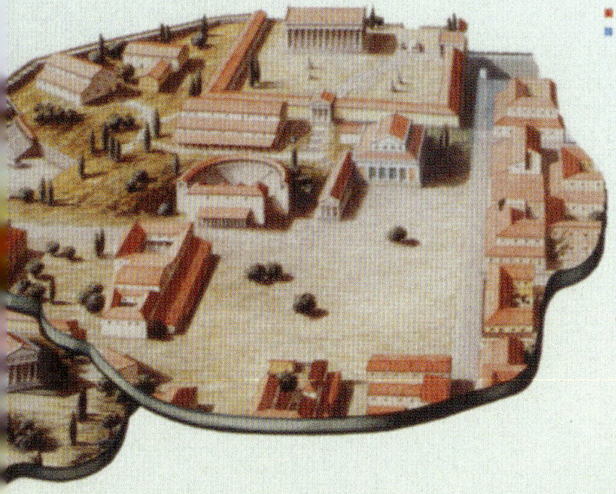

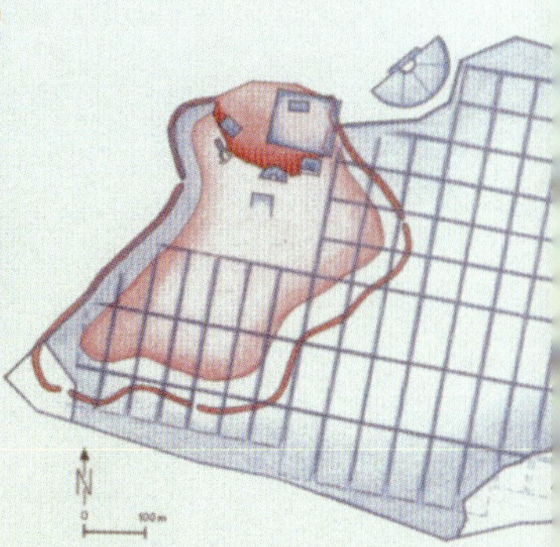

The Homeric Troia

■ Troia VI: Citadel and Lower City with fortification ditch
■ Troia IX: (Ilium): Acropolis and Lower City with street plan

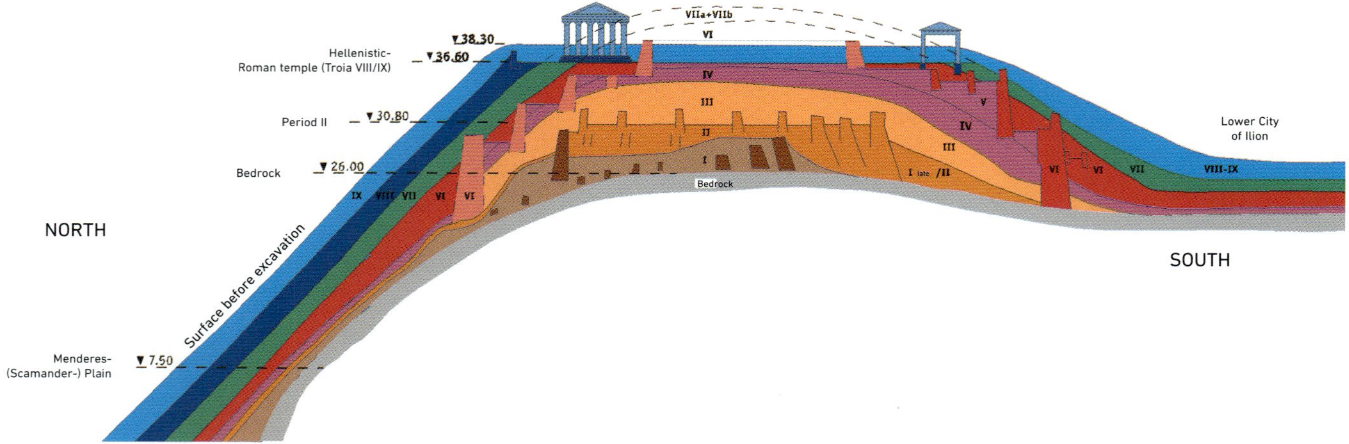

Fig. 35 Schematic cross-section of Hisarlık (Troia) showing the nine different periods.

The ten "cities" of Troia, from the oldest upward

Troia I-III, the Trojan Maritime Culture (ca. 2920-2200 BCE)

This culture spread along the coasts and nearby islands in both the Aegean and the Sea of Marmara, as evidenced by both commercial and cultural influence. The latter can be traced into the Mediterranean region (as far as Malta), southeastern Europe (Bulgaria), Asia Minor (most particularly the area of Eskişehir), and as far eastward as central Asia (Afghanistan).

Troia I (ca. 2920-2350 BCE = Early Bronze Age II), the earliest settlement (Fig. 38), comprises a total of 14 building phases; it boasted –in spite of its still rustic character– an enclosure wall of fieldstone, reinforced and renovated several times over. The main gate in the south, fortified with rectangular bastions (Fig. 39), thus figures as one of the most important gates in Asia Minor. In the "Schliemann-Trench," a row of long houses was exposed (Figs. 40, 94-96), one of which –House Number 102– may be considered (on the basis of plan and dimensions) an early representative of the ***megaron***. The populace supported themselves through agriculture and husbandry as well as fishing. The pottery was entirely handmade, with surface colors ranging from dark brown to black, some vessels decorated with white-filled incision (Fig. 90).

Troia II (ca. 2550-2250 = Early Bronze Age II) clearly represents a citadel indicative of a ruling class with far-reaching contacts. A mudbrick fortification wall 330 m. in circumference was built on sloping stone foundations reaching as high as six meters, surrounding a citadel of nearly 9,000 m^2 (Fig. 41). Within this upper city, we see clearly planned and well-built ***megara*** (long slim structures with a front porch enclosed at either side, the forerunner of

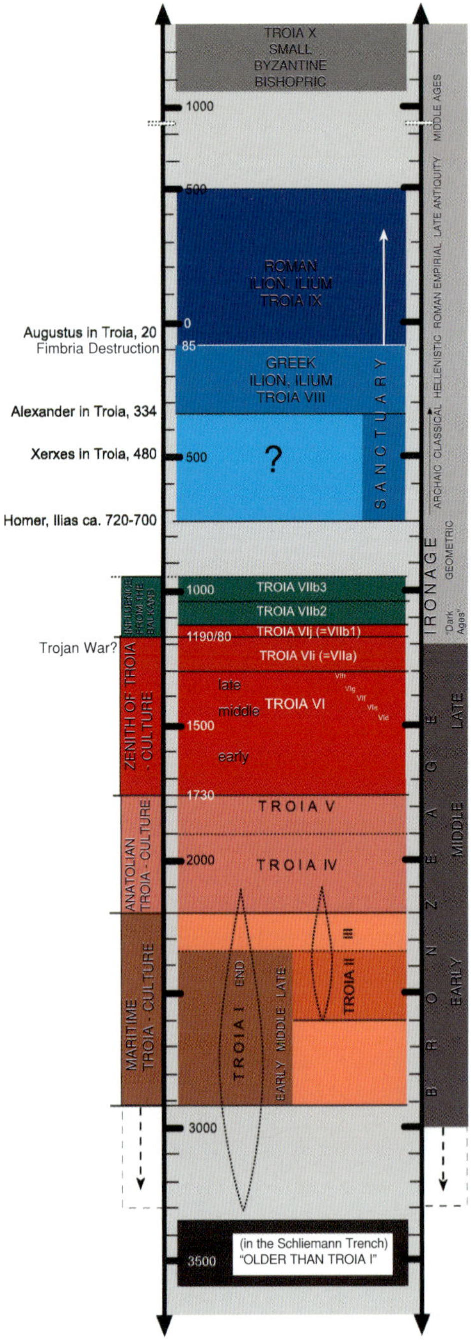

Fig. 36
Chronological sequence on the citadel at Hisarlık (Troia).

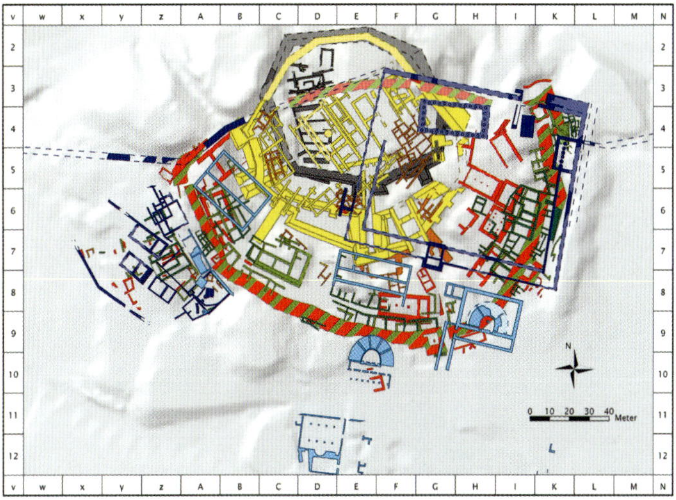

Fig. 37 Composite phase plan of the citadel (Troia I-IX).

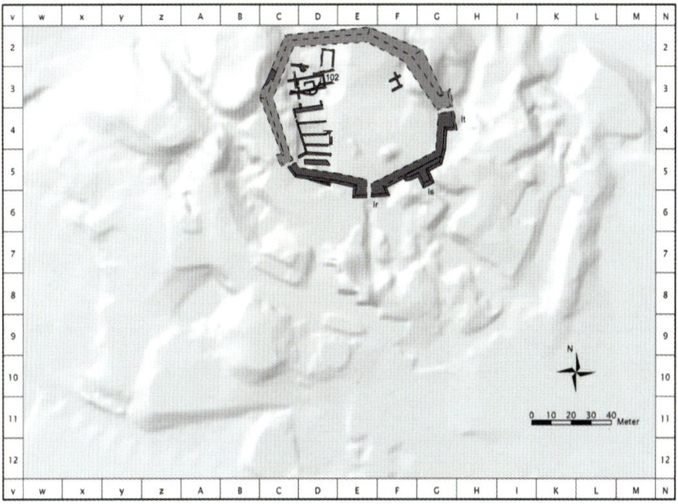

Fig. 38 Troia I (Early Bronze Age, ca. 2920-2350 BCE), with the earliest remains from the Schliemann-Trench (ca. 2920-2800) indicated in black.

Fig. 39 The fortification wall and the eastern portion of the tower at the South Gate (Early Troia I-Middle Troia I). Early Bronze Age, ca. 2920-2600 BCE. From the south.

Fig. 40
Stone foundations of long houses from Early Troia I (ca. 2920-2800) in the Schliemann-Trench. From the north.

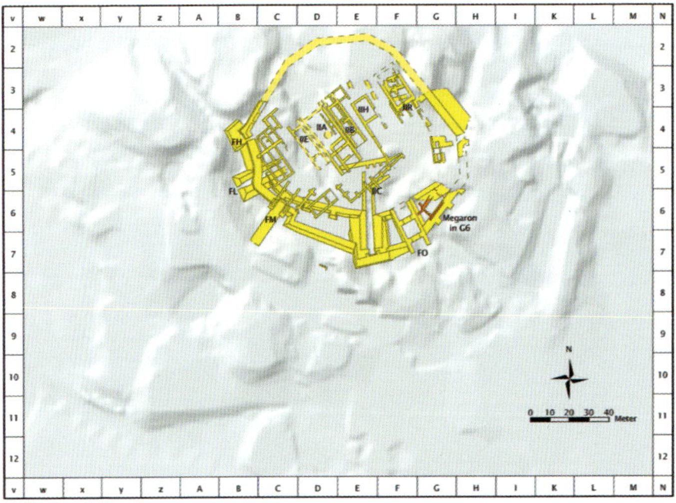

Fig. 41 The citadel of Troia II (Early Bronze Age, ca. 2550-2250 BCE).

Fig. 42 Reconstruction of the Troia II citadel (© Ch. Haußner).

the Greek temple *in antis*); these most probably represented shrines –they must have served as foci for public gatherings (Fig. 42). The entrance to these structures, surrounded by roofed colonnades, was through a monumental gate (Propylon II). Other entrances to the citadel were through other likewise impressive gates at the southeast and southwest, the latter approached by a steep paved ramp (Fig. 43) with a parapet (partially restored). More than 20 "treasures" including Schliemann's "Treasure of Priam" (Fig. 99), have been discovered in and above the burned ruins of the palaces and public structures of Troia II. Three

Fig. 43 The fortification wall of Troia II (ca. 2550-2250 BCE) with the paved ramp leading to the Southwest Gate. In the background appears the sail-like roofing above the megaron in Quadrat G 6.

Fig. 44
The foundation trench of the outer palisade of Troia II (ca. 2550-2250 BCE) cut into the bedrock. From the southwest.

great conflagrations have been attested during the eight or so phases of the period. Finds attest trade to all points of the compass; outstanding is the immaculate craftsmanship otherwise known only in Mesopotamia and Egypt at this early a date. Tin –a prerequisite for molding bronze artifacts (including weapons that were obviously a great asset in warfare)– appears to have been plentiful at Troia and must have been imported from a great distance, perhaps as far abroad as central Asia. Particularly surprising here is the frequent use of the potter's wheel, a technique foreign to the region; most Trojan wheelmade pottery was manufactured in yellowish and pinkish buff wares (Fig 92). Tall

Fig. 45 Virtual reconstruction of the palisade in perspective.

Fig. 46 Vessel with a "face-lid" (Troia IV).

Fig. 47 The double-handled goblet known as the depas amphikypellon.

slender goblets –suggesting viticulture and wineries– with pointed bases and two opposing handles (the so-called "depas amphikypellon", Fig. 47) are very common.

The "Burnt City" is indeed one of the most impressive monuments in prehistoric archaeology –so impressive that Schliemann at first took it to represent the Troia/Ilios of the ***Iliad***. During the progress of the excavations, however, he eventually realized his mistake and admitted it not long before his decease. Today we know that some 1250 years lay between the "Burnt City" of Troia II and the time of the Trojan War.

At the southern foot of the citadel lay a lower city of an approximated 90,000 m^2, surrounded by a wooden palisade (Figs. 44, 45). Surviving today are only the foundations of this bulwark preserved as a negative impression cut into bedrock near one of the gates.

Troia III (ca. 2250-2200 = Early Bronze Age II) is represented by an inventory of finds generally resembling those of Troia II and implying cultural continuity. Structures on the citadel grew smaller and more numerous during

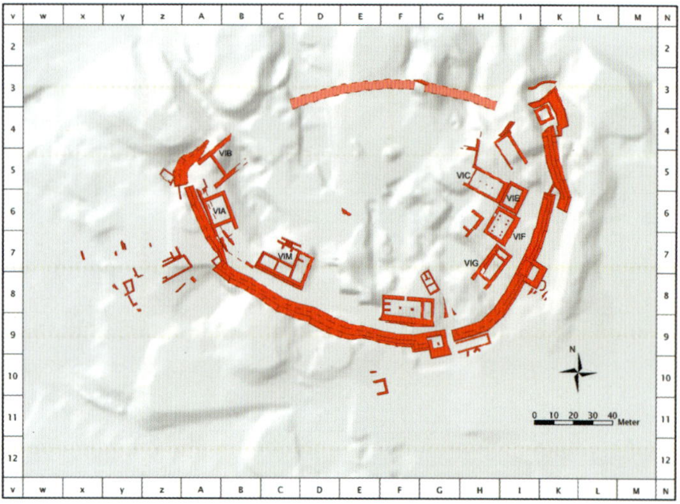

Fig. 48 Troia VI (Middle and Late Bronze Ages, 17th -13th centuries BCE).

the four or so phases of this settlement; these followed quickly upon one another and ended in a fiery destruction. Although the above suggests comparatively straitened circumstances, we cannot rule out the possibility that some of the "treasures" belonged to this period.

Troia IV/V, the Anatolian-Trojan Culture
(ca. 2200-1740/30 BCE)

Troia IV and Troia V (ca. 2200-1740/30 BCE = Early Bronze III and the beginnings of the Middle Bronze Age) saw a gradual expansion of the citadel to some 18,000 m^2. Troia IV is represented by seven phases, each destroyed by fire, and Troia V can also be divided into several building levels. In Troia IV we see an economy based more strongly on hunting, with finds indicating a pronounced influence from inland Anatolia (although there is no marked break in the ceramic tradition). Typical of the pottery inventory are vessels portraying the human face (Fig. 46) and the so-called "depas amphikypellon" (Fig. 47). Inside the houses, now built side-by-side to support a common roof (typical of the Anatolian Settlement Plan), we now find

Fig. 49 Late Bronze Age remains from Troia VI (15th-13th cent. BCE). Aerial view from the east showing a tower and stretch of the citadel fortifications enclosing the palaces.

domed ovens, which also suggest a change in palate and dietary habit. The final phase of Troia V was destroyed in a conflagration.

Troia VI, the Zenith of Trojan Culture
(ca. 1740/30- 1180 BCE)

Troia VI (ca. 1740/30-1300 BCE = Middle to Late Bronze Age), presumably the setting of Homer's Troia/

Fig. 50 Aerial photograph of Troia. From the north.

Fig. 51 The East Tower and East Gate of Troia VI (Late Bronze Age, 15th-13th cent. BCE).

(W)Ilios and perhaps Taru(w)isa or Wilusa, the main phase of the golden age at the site, can be described as both a thriving city and a place of trade. Firstly, impressive palatial residences on completely new lines stood on an enlarged fortified citadel of some 20,000 m^2 (Fig. 48). This new citadel was grander probably not only in scale but in significance as well –larger than any previously discovered at Hisarlık– or anywhere else within a 100-km radius. As part and parcel of the political system in the eastern Mediterranean, the city was obviously of great strategic importance because of the geographical location. A sloping fortification wall of dressed stone replete with towers and bastions encircled the citadel, ca. 180 x 125 m. (Figs. 49-51). These foundations were four to five meters in breadth, with a height of more than six meters; crowned with a mudbrick superstructure, the wall stood most likely some ten meters high. Particularly of note are the "saw-tooth" offsets and certain stretches of the wall with masonry displaying a slight curvature (presumably a precaution against earthquakes). Several gates and doorways led into the citadel, with the main entrance from the south, guarded by a tower; ***stelai*** (upright stone blocks) stood before it (Fig. 53). A paved street led upward to the buildings within, arranged upon concentric terraces. Monumental freestanding structures, some two-storied and some representing the megaron

Fig. 52 Detail of masonry from Palace VI M in the off-set technique, Troia VI (Late Bronze Age, 15th-13 cent. BCE). From the Dörpfeld Archives at the German Archaeological Institute in Athens (no. 559).

Fig. 53 The South Gate of Troia VI (Late Bronze Age, 15th-13th cent. BCE). From the south. Note the tower with the stelai (upright stones) before it, as well as the drainage canal under the street.

form, were found preserved only on the outermost terrace of the citadel –just within the defense wall (Fig. 49). Of particular significance are Houses VI E (with steeply rising exterior walls of dressed stone) and VI F (with stone footers for vertical supports and recesses for horizontal beams). Of note as well is the originally two-storied 'L'-shaped House VI M on sloping foundations with offsets –and Megaron VI A in the very west. These must have been individual palatial residences.

The central palace must have stood high at the center, but all remains here were cleared away when the third-century Temple of Athena was constructed (Troia VIII). The whole of the imposing citadel –doubtless the project of a respected magistrate– was excavated by Dörpfeld, who identified it as the Homeric Troia/Ilios of the 13th century BCE.

The final phase of these strata fell prey to a catastrophic earthquake.

Fig. 54 Entrance to the lower city of Troia VI (Late Bronze Age, ca. 1400-1300 BCE). Here you see the defensive ditch cut into the bedrock as well as the foundations of Hellenistic houses.

One focus of the Troia Project as renewed in 1988 has been the search for a contemporary –second millennium BCE– lower city. Such has indeed been located: south of the acropolis and bordered by a 'U'-shaped ditch found cut into the bedrock (apparently intended to ward off chariot attacks), stretching as far as 400 m south of the citadel walls (Fig. 54).

The NW quarter of the lower city has been exposed over a large area, and in other soundings enough architecture has come to light that we may assume a fairly dense population throughout the settlement, which represents (including the citadel as well) a good 300,000 m^2. The entire population can thus be estimated at around 7000.

Remains of a contemporary necropolis with both cremation burials in urns and inhumations have been located outside the defense ditch (some 550 m south of the citadel walls). A similar cemetery has been discovered at Beşik Bay some eight kilometers SW of Troia, dating to this same period –ending in an earthquake followed by a century of political upheaval.

Further discovered was an artificial water-cave established as early as the third millennium BCE. This –as well as other finds– clearly speaks for the identification of the site as the Hittite vassal state Wilusa. The idea that Troia/Wilusa had played an active role in the dominant culture of the second millennium BCE was first suggested as early as 1924 by the Austrian scholar Paul Kretschmer and has been even more strongly supported over the last decade by leading scholars of language and history (independent of the archaeological evidence).

Characteristic among the ceramics of the period is a fine and lustrous gray burnished ware that is found as an occasional import in Greece and even as far abroad as Cyprus and the Levant; such pottery has been interpreted as imitation of silver vessels. Newly and quite well represented among the animal bones recovered from this phase is that of the horse, which played an important role in warfare (the chariot!) from the beginning of the second millennium BCE onwards. Intensive trade and cultural exchange is obvious, not only from the wide-ranging ceramic repertoire, but from small finds in ivory and ostrich shell, accompanied as well by beads of carnelian and faience. That these finds both mirror and are mirrored by the dynamic image of the city once again indicates its strategic location. Trade in metal was doubtless the spring in the works that brought such prosperity; from molds found on the site, we know that metals were smelted here. There is much that is left to the imagination as well, the conveniences of the time: the horses, perishable wood and textiles, and –of course– the slaves and servants. Foreign trade seems to have been flourishing towards the end of the phase, as is clear from the ever-increasing quantity of Mycaenean ceramics, for example.

Late Troia VI and Troia VIi (the latter formerly known as Troia VII a), yield finds that indicate a cultural unity. Following the seismic catastrophe, the population returned; now the position of Troia in a power-play between the Achaeans (Thebans?) and the Hittites (based in their Central Anatolian capital of Hattusha) escalated. The Trojans were constantly busied with construction and defense. Provisions were stockpiled and treaties signed. Throughout the region, the 13th century seems to have been an epoch of constant activity and stress. Dörpfeld himself regretted his original arbitrary division of phases and later suggested renaming VIIa as VIi (as well as perhaps labeling VII b1 as VIj). Because our recent excavations confirm these later thoughts of his, we have adopted his suggestions even though the American excavator Blegen had retained the designation of Troia VIIa (our Troia VIi destroyed by fire) for Homer's Ilios.

Troia VIi, formerly Troia VIIa (ca. 1300-1180 BCE = Late Bronze Age, the strata most likely to have been Homer's Troia/ (W)Ilios and Taru(w)isa or Wilusa), was a settlement built upon the ruins of the preceding period of Troia VI (apparently destroyed by an earthquake). That it was restored by the same population is clear. Whatever could be salvaged from earlier structures was reused –in

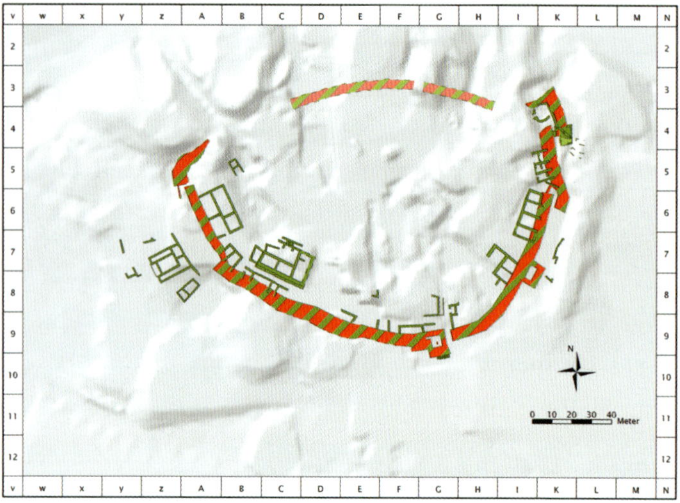

Fig. 55 Troia VI i (= VII a), Late Bronze Age (13th-early 12th cent. BCE).

particular the fortifications; new additions include streets and towers (Figs. 49, 51, 53, 55). The archaeological finds do not seem to demonstrate any setback whatsoever; to the contrary, the economy apparently continued to flourish. A note of tension pervaded the settlement, however; the citadel was outfitted with storage facilities, for example, and certain entrances were walled up. Settlement in both the upper and lower cities was denser than before, though still following a systematical layout. This development was accompanied by an apparent desertion of the outlying areas, with the cemetery near Beşik Bay falling out of use as well. Considering the ecology of the age, the population could not have exceeded 10,000.

It was at least another century before the city of Troia once again suffered destruction, this time (ca. 1180 BCE) most probably at the hands of an invading enemy.

Troia VIj / formerly designated as Troia VIIb1 (ca. 1180-1130 BCE), a period transitional to the Early Iron Age, constitutes a short transitional phase in which we see some continuation of the earlier culture mixed with elements of a simpler tradition. It most likely represents the take-over of the site by a population culturally akin to the earlier inhabitants. Together with the wheelmade pottery, we suddenly observe a large quantity of simple handmade wares that –although perhaps local– had not been in evidence at Troia itself for centuries. The rebuilding at the site reflects the efforts of an obviously "humble folk" –yet one that nevertheless might have seen themselves as "Trojans." This phase ended with a partial destruction of the site.

Troia VIIb2-3, a Trojan Culture with some influence from the Balkans (ca. 1150-950 BCE = Early Iron Age)

In Phases 2 and 3 of Troia VIIb (Fig. 56) we witness the appearance of certain elements definitely distinct from those familiar to the site. In addition to the wheelmade wares, we now see handmade ceramics familiar from the northeastern Balkans and the western Black Sea coast –vessels ornamented with channeling and bosses. The architecture, characterized by small units, is concentrated in the upper city and the immediate surroundings. Phase VIIb2 is distinguished by the use

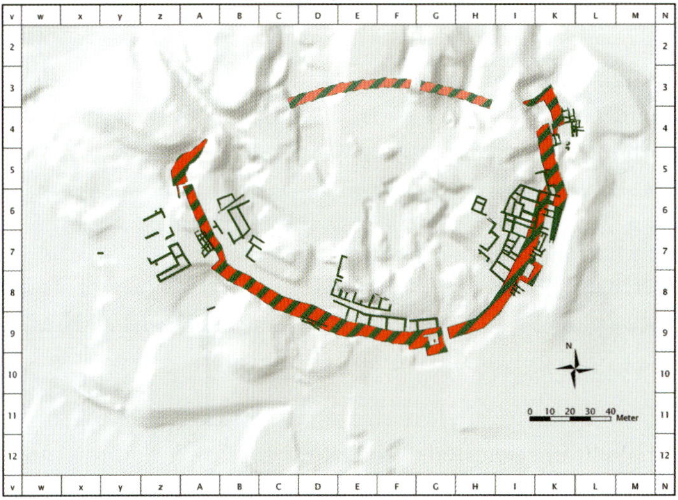

Fig. 56 Troia VII b (Early Iron Age, 12th -10th cent. BCE).

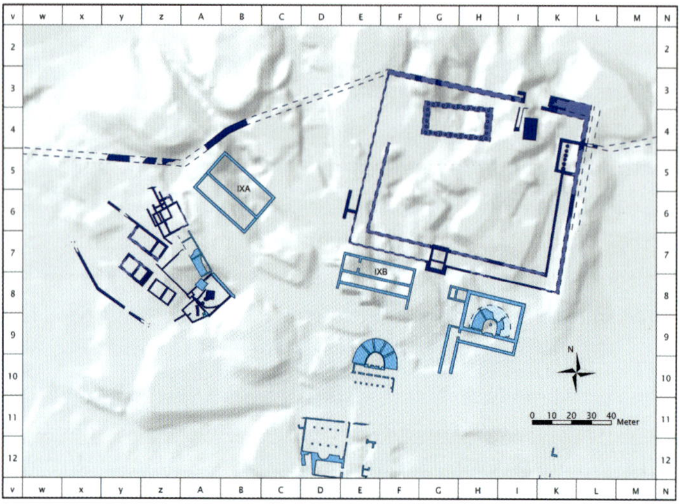

Fig. 57 Late Troia VIII (the Hellenistic Ilion, shown in dark blue) and Troia IX (the Roman Ilium, in light blue).

of somewhat irregular orthostats (vertical stone slabs) lining the lower walls, and the existence of at least one further phase (VII b 3) has been confirmed in the recent excavations.

Hiatus ? (ca. 950-720/700 BCE)

During these 250 years Troia was only sparsely –if at all– inhabited. This, of course, does not rule out the possibility of rites continuing in a sanctuary upon the citadel. Although the site must have appeared rather desolate, the late Bronze Age fortifications at least would have retained their majesty.

Troia VIII, the Greek Ilion
(ca. 700-85 BCE = Archaic through Hellenistic times)

The earliest structures representing a sanctuary at the nearly deserted site are those established by the Aeolian Greeks sometime after 700 BCE, thus apparently existing within the lifetime of Homer! Votive offerings confirm the existence of much earlier sacred precincts as well.

Following centuries of modest subsistence, the Trojan cult bloomed again in the third century BCE, when a temple of Athena on the acropolis was consecrated in honor of the "Sacred City of Ilion," the site of the Trojan War. Further sanctuaries and temples sprang up westward (Fig. 57). Although little was preserved of the main temple aside from scattered architectural members in marble and the rectangular foundation of the altar; the impressive walls of the *temenos*, the holy precinct encompassing a rectangular area of 9,500 m^2, and the foundations of the long stoas lining them are still to be traced (Fig. 58). Before or during the construction of this temple to Athena, the high centrally located structures of Troia VI and VII had been razed, thus erasing most clues to the character of the Bronze-Age citadel (cf. Fig. 35).

Ilion became the religious and political capital of a federation of municipalities, and to the south and east of the acropolis a lower city (on a grid-plan) arose –overtop and partially dug into remains from Troia VI/VII (Fig. 59). Toward the end of the third century BCE, this lower settlement was enclosed by a wall 3.6 km in length.

Fig. 58 Reconstruction of the Roman Ilium (Troia IX). © Ch. Haußner.

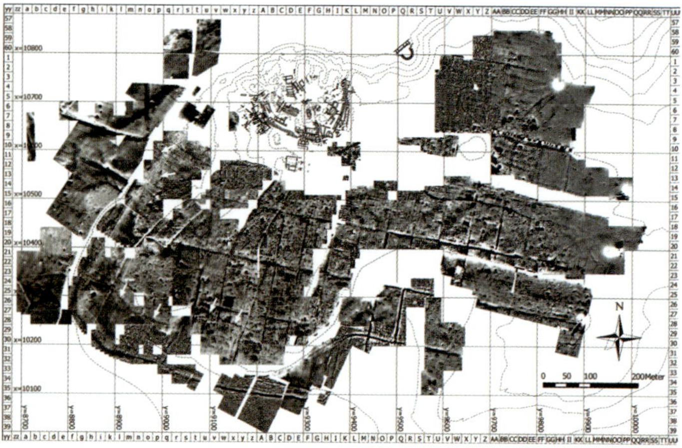

Fig. 59 Geomagnetics reveals much; here you can see not only the regular rectangular blocks (insulae) of the Greek and Roman lower settlements, but the limits of the prehistoric settlement as well (the defensive ditch in the west and south, indicated by white arrows).

Fig. 60
A statue of Emperor Hadrian found in the Odeion of Roman Ilium (Troia IX).

Then in 85 BCE the disloyal and conniving Roman general Fimbria sacked the "Sacred City of Ilion."

Troia IX, the Roman Ilium (85 BCE-ca. 500 CE)

Emperor Augustus, who was proud to trace his genealogy to Troia (through his reputed ancestor Aeneas), restored the Trojan Temple of Athena. Throughout all of Ilium efforts of restoration and rebuilding were undertaken: among the latter was an odeion (later repaired by the Roman emperors Hadrian and Caracalla; Figs. 60, 116), a nearby gymnasium and bath complex (?) from which a few mosaic floors have survived, and a large theater in the natural depression northeast of the temple (Figs. 76, 77). Throughout the third century CE, donations continued to pour into Ilium; new public edifices graced the acropolis, and the lower city –typified by the ***insula*** ("island" or "building-block") system– developed further within its own enclosure walls (Figs. 59, 61, 62). Urban development then dwindled off to a halt around 500 CE, victimized by at least two severe earthquakes.

Fig. 61 A street in the lower city of Roman Ilium (Troia IX). Quadrat I 17, from the west.

The early fourth century again saw some new construction in the city, which had in fact represented the first choice of Constantine the Great for his new capital in the Eastern Roman Empire.

Fresh water for the Roman Ilium was provided from the foothills of Mount Ida through clay pipes and aqueducts (Fig. 63).

The majority of Roman burials have appeared toward the southeast of the city.

Troia X, Byzantine Ilion (primarily the 12th and 13th centuries CE)

As early as the fourth century Ilion was the seat of a bishopric; after the seismic destruction ca. 500 CE, however, the first expansion of new settlement is represented by remains from the late 12th century located in the west near the Greco-Roman Sanctuary. Indirect evidence of the increase in population is provided by the many burials found scattered throughout the earlier settlement, but concentrated primarily around the great theater to the north and the water-cave to the southwest. It was the Ottoman

Fig. 62 Excavation in the lower city of Roman Ilium (Troia IX). Here, too, the rock-cut foundations for the palisade of Troia II are visible.

conquest of the territory in the mid-fourteenth century that brought this chapter of history to a close.

Troia Today

In 1996 the Turkish Republic set the immediate landscape aside as a new national park, the "Historical National Park of Troia" (Fig. 31). As a consequence, all the surroundings you gaze upon on this visit to the citadel (an area of some 12 x 12 km) are under special protection. Upon a proposal of the Turkish government, the ruins of Troia were accepted into UNESCO's "World Heritage" list of sites outstanding in the history of mankind, an honor that deserves and demands a fair share of responsibility.

The number of visitors to the site is expected to reach half a million per year by 2013 or 2014.

Each year during the summer months some 60 archaeologists and scientists from more than ten different countries gather to work at Troia.

We may all now thankfully proclaim, "Troia lives on –there are some among us looking after the site!"

Fig. 63 An aqueduct east of the city that served Roman Ilium (Troia IX).

7. (Info Panel B) The Pithos Garden

The Pithos

The large (tall, slender and somewhat barrel-shaped) storage vessels known as pithoi represent one of the earliest shapes typical of Mediterranean and Near Eastern pottery (Fig. 64). The pithos provided not only cool and safe storage for olive oil, wine, and grain, but served in nautical transport as well. Often as tall as a man, these thick-walled vessels are frequently found half-buried in the earth of pantries and storerooms (explaining why they are typically pointed at the bottom with no flat base upon which to stand). Discarded pithoi sometimes lined the edges of wells, and –from the Early Bronze Age onward– were often "recycled" as burial urns.

Fig. 64
Large storage vessels in Megaron VI A (Late Bronze Age, 15th-13th cent. BCE). From the Dörpfeld Archives at the German Archaeological Institute in Athens (no. 280).

Ceramic Water Pipes

The Roman architect and writer Vitruvius, who elucidated nearly every detail of contemporary building in his work ***De Architectura***, discussed water pipes in Chapter vi of Book VII, which describes three methods for channeling water: stone channels, lead pipes, and pipes of clay. Of the three, he recommended pipes of clay (Fig. 65) as being easier to produce and more economical than stone, and much better for health than those of lead. The sturdy clay pipes found at Troia, articulated to fit one inside the next, correspond to his recommendations –and resemble as well many other water pipes found throughout the Roman world. The joints were sealed with a mixture of slaked lime and oil. Bends and bifurcations were usually facilitated by units chiseled from stone.

Fig. 65 Clay pipes employed in Troia IX (Roman Ilium).

Grinding Stones and Pestles

The cereal grains represent one of the very earliest foods in the human diet. Seeds of wild grasses gathered in the surroundings had always provided a source of nourishment, and it was probably the grains that were first selected for planting and reaping some 10,000 years ago at the very beginnings of the Neolithic settled economy; they very soon became a staple. Before the harvested grain could be used, however, it had to be hulled and ground.

Threshing sleds and basins for stamping came into play –as well as grinding stones (the latter remaining in use through recent times). To facilitate storage and preservation, only as much grain as required would be cracked or pulverized shortly before use; this meant at least one grindstone for each household. Over the centuries these articles have remained practically unaltered in form. Grain is scattered over the surface of a flat or saddle-shaped grinding stone and energetically stroked with a hand-held pestle (generally ovoid or cylindrical in form).

To achieve a relatively fine flour-like substance, both stones employed must be rough in texture, yet hard and resistant –the latter to minimize the amount of grit in the resulting product. Granite, basalt, and porphyry were used whenever available. Such hand-mills represented standard practice until the practical "turnstile" mill was eventually introduced in Mesopotamia ca. 1000 BCE, reaching some outlying regions only one millennium later.

It seems to have been the girls and women of antiquity who were primarily responsible for this long and exhausting process. This is suggested not only by ancient Egyptian frescoes, but also by morphological alteration in the joints of female skeletal evidence.

THE AREA DEDICATED TO OUR SPONSORS

8. The Eternal Stone of Troia

Dr. Süleyman Bodur, one of the Friends of Troia, was struck with a very thoughtful inspiration. It is to him that we owe this special monument, a 20-ton dressed block of granite (Fig. 66). Upon this, a list of mentors and sponsors has been engraved for future generations.

It is most significant that Troia was one of the earliest sites on the border of Asia and Europe to employ dressed stone masonry of smooth rectangular blocks –and this in the Bronze Age, a period that did not know even the use of iron. The first such masonry you see is that in Megaron II A (ca. 2500 BCE). It is followed by the "well-hewn stones" of the fortification wall, palaces, and houses in the lower city of Troia during the second millennium BCE. Troia should be remembered not only for early progress in metallurgy (tin-bronze), ceramics (the potter's wheel) and city planning (citadel + lower city), but also for an architecture outstanding for in its time.

This dedicatory stone was presented in the summer of 2002 to the Troia Foundation as a gift of Dr. Süleyman Bodur from the firm TROAS Minerals A.Ş. in Çan.

Fig. 66
The granite block established by Dr. Süleyman Bodur to honor the sponsors of Troia.

WITHIN THE RUINS OF TROIA

9. (Info Panel 1b) History of the Discovery and Excavation of Troia

The successful businessman Heinrich Schliemann (Fig. 67), after long perusal of the *Iliad*, found himself fully convinced that the Troia (W)Ilios of Homer lay beneath the Roman settlement visible on the 150 x 200 m-mound of Hisarlık (= fortified mound) just south of the straits of the Dardanelles (the Hellespont) on a limestone tableland between the rivers of the Scamander (Kara Menderes) and the Simois (Dümrek), only 4.5 km from the Dardanelles and six kilometers from the Aegean Coast, and therefore in a most strategic position (Figs. 29-31). Frank Calvert, who had taken up residence in the area, had already concluded that Hisarlık was a settlement mound representing many centuries of deposit; he had even opened some small sondages (1863-1865) with the conviction that the Troia celebrated by Homer lay here.

Fig. 67
Heinrich Schliemann (6.1.1822-26.12.1890) at the age of 58.

The First Nine Campaigns

From 1871 to 1894 (following preliminary sondages in 1870) the first nine excavation campaigns took place with magnanimous effort. Schliemann, who invested large sums from his private estate to the cause, remained in charge until 1890; he immediately pronounced Troia II, where he believed he had found the "Treasure of Priam," the Troia of the ***Iliad***. After Schliemann's decease, the architect Wilhelm Dörpfeld (Fig. 68), his assistant and architect for the project, continued in 1893 and 1894. It was Dörpfeld who exposed the impressive fortifications of Troia VI, which he then interpreted as "the Homeric Troia."

Schliemann was an individual with many interests, "possessed" by some of them, and his relationships with others, as well as with his finds –the "Treasure" in particular– has led to various condemnations. Looking back today, we may justify some of this criticism, for it appears that he was on one hand a dedicated scholar, but on the other a "treasure-seeker" who illicitly spirited valuable finds out of the country.

These early campaigns represented the first step into a new era of methodical archaeological excavation. We should thus be neither too surprised nor too critical that some significant contexts were inadvertently overlooked and lost. During his work in Troia Schliemann quickly learned to separate individual strata and distinguish diagnostic forms among the pottery

Fig. 68
Wilhelm Dörpfeld (26.12.1853-25.4.1940), probably around 85 years of age.

so richly represented in them. Truly cooperating with him in deed as well as word were the Consul Frank Calvert (scholar and collector), Rudolph Virchow (pathologist, anthropologist and prehistorian), and Wilhelm Dörpfeld (architect).

The successive building levels were numbered I - IX from the lowest upward; for this perceptive division we must thank the careful observation of Dörpfeld. Even in these early days, a fair share of scientific scholarship was introduced –and a fine example for future archaeologists was also set by a thorough survey of the surroundings during these early campaigns at Hisarlık. Trenches were opened at Pasha Tepe, Beşik-Sivritepe and other tumuli (burial mounds), as well as soundings at the settlement mounds of Hanay Tepe and Karaağaç Tepe.

The excavations at Troia awakened a new enthusiasm for archaeological "digs" in the public eye, and the experience gained in the Schliemann Excavations opened the way for true discipline in archaeological fieldwork. Even today the results of these early campaigns remain the basis for continuing work at the site as well as a keystone for other excavations, particularly those in northwestern Turkey and the bordering regions.

The majority of the finds from the first nine campaigns were distributed among the Museums of Istanbul, Athens, and Berlin. For educational purposes, close "twins" among the more than 10,000 objects taken to Berlin were then distributed among museums and university collections throughout Europe. The most outstanding pieces from Berlin were taken to Moscow and St. Petersburg during World War II; many of those remaining, of course, were lost or damaged in the war (ca. 50%). Today, finds from these early campaigns are spread over some 50 museums and collections worldwide.

In 1924, small-scale excavations in the area of Beşik Bay were undertaken by Wilhelm Dörpfeld, Oscar Mey and Martin Schede. There on the coastline, today silted up, lay the Aegean harbor of Troia. Investigated as well were the neighboring tumuli of Üvecik Tepe and Beşik-Sivritepe.

The Tenth through Sixteenth Campaigns

These next seven campaigns at Troia took place between 1932 and 1938 under the leadership of Carl W. Blegen (Fig. 69) and the University of Cincinnati (USA). With improved excavation techniques and methods, the team was able to subdivide the phases into a total of 46 building levels. Blegen identified Level VII a (now reevaluated as Level VI i) with the city of the Trojan War. During these campaigns as well, investigation in the surroundings continued (including excavation at Kumtepe undertaken in cooperation with Hâmit Zübeyr Koşay, as well as at Karajur Tepe, Ballı Dağ, and Eski Hisarlık).

The finds from these seven campaigns are housed in the Archaeological Museums of Istanbul and Çanakkale.

Following a year of survey (1981) in the area, from 1982 to 1987, excavation in the north of the now silted-up Beşik Bay was undertaken by Manfred Korfmann (Tübingen University). Investigated during these annual campaigns were the sites of Beşik-Sivritepe, Beşik-Yassıtepe and a cemetery discovered on the shores of the former bay.

Fig. 69
Carl William Blegen (27.1.1887-24.8.1971), probably in his early 60's.

The Seventeenth Campaign Onward

After a break of 50 years, excavation at Troia was renewed in 1988 by an international team of Turks, Germans, and Americans coordinated by Manfred Korfmann (Figs. 70, 71). Each and every summer further "digging" has taken place; therefore many finds included here represent our most recent discoveries (reported annually in the journal ***Studia Troica***). Most of the evidence from classical antiquity (the Greek and Roman periods) has been brought to light and evaluated by C. Brian Rose from the University of Cincinnati. By the end of the 2004 campaign nearly 400 scholars and technicians from 20 different countries had participated (supported by some 50-100 local staff as well). We are faced, therefore, with an immense quantity of finds to evaluate and publish. The number of scholarly publications produced by our participants (as of 2004) has been most impressive, totaling around 180 articles representing ca. 6000 pages of text.

Fig. 70 The international excavation team of 2003.

All finds from these recent campaigns are housed in the Archaeological Museum of Çanakkale.

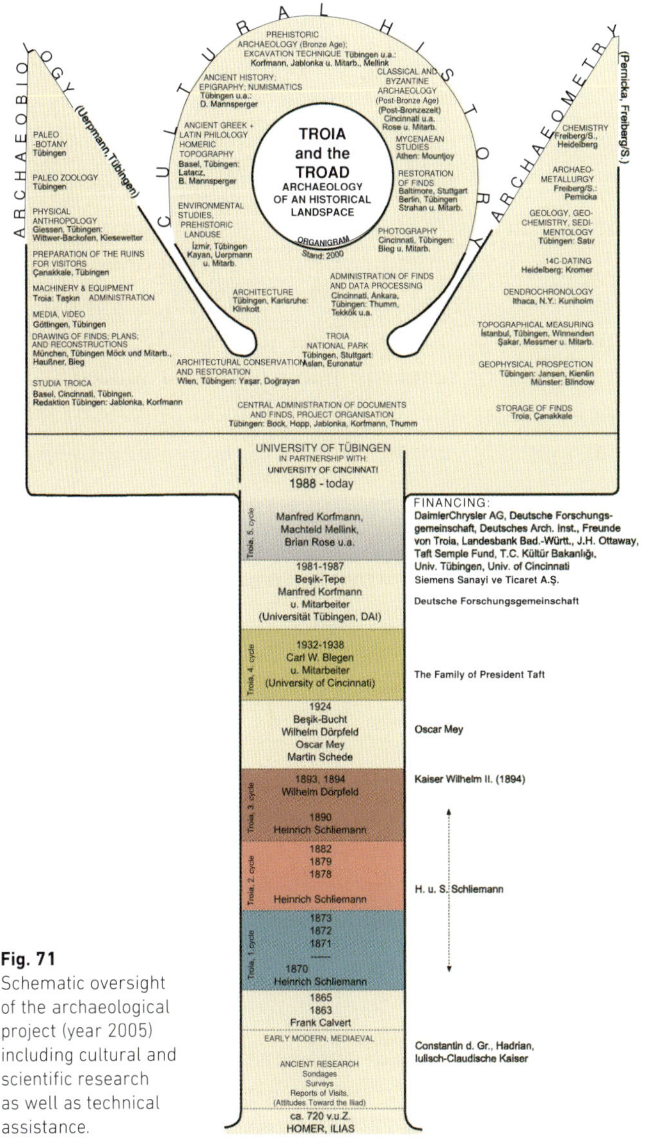

Fig. 71
Schematic oversight of the archaeological project (year 2005) including cultural and scientific research as well as technical assistance.

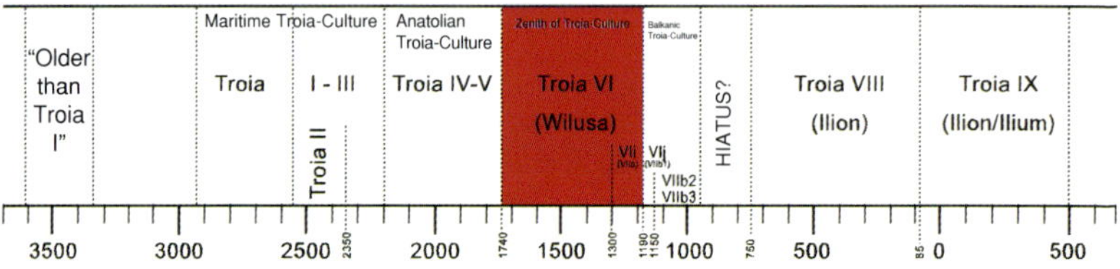

10. (Info Panel 2) The East Wall – Troia VI

You are now standing upon remains of the outer wall of the Greek and Roman Temple Precinct (Troia VIII / IX, 3rd century BCE – ca. 500 CE). Before you lie the citadel fortifications of Troia/Ilios. You can easily identify the East Tower and the East Wall (with an entranceway), behind which you see the "palaces" of the Late Troia VI period (ca. 1430 - 1300 BCE). Atop the fortifications remain a few traces of houses from Troia VII as well. Troia VI was destroyed around 1300 BCE –apparently by an earthquake– while the cities of VI i (= the former VII a, renamed because of cultural continuity) and VII b both met fiery ends, with the conflagration marking the end of Troia VI i dated ca. 1180 BCE.

Behind you lies the lower city of Greco-Roman Ilion. To the north, you see the Dardanelles and the plain of the Kara Menderes (the ancient River Scamander) stretching away to the west. On a clear day you may glimpse the peaks of the Kaz Dağları (the range of Mount Ida) to the southeast, and in the southwest a burial mound (the tumulus of Üvecik Tepe) at the edge of the low basin that was once the Aegean harbor of Troia (Beşik Bay). On the horizon, then, appears the island Bozcaada –the ancient Greek Tenedos (Figs. 30, 31).

The East Wall and the East Gate

The circumference of these citadel fortifications measured some 550 m, of which only about 330 m are still visible today.

With its regular and well-hewn blocks of limestone, the segment of the ring wall before you is a masterwork of architecture (Fig. 49). The shallow vertical setbacks in the sloping façade (Fig. 52) would have provided a visual complement to the square beams within and at the base of the timber-frame construction of the sun-dried mudbrick superstructure that crowned these stone revetments. The stone foundations –4.5-5.0 m wide– rise to a height of six meters, and the superstructure probably rose another three or four meters. In a later phase, the mudbrick superstructure was replaced by a stone wall of light construction (Figs. 49, 51). The overlap created by two sections of the fortification wall running parallel to one another here formed a well-protected entranceway. As early as the Hellenistic period, deep cuttings for the terracing and precinct walls of the Athena temenos had been made in the eastern flank.

The East Tower

This massive tower added to the East Wall in a later phase (probably in the 13th century BCE), displays exceptionally fine construction (Figs. 49-51). Eleven meters wide, it projected eight meters from the wall with an eastern façade three meters deep. Wooden flooring divided the tower into two stories, with access only from the upper floor.

The "Palaces"

The radially oriented Palaces VI E and VI F (Figs. 48, 49) consist of large single rooms (64 and 98 m^2 respectively) surrounded by walls one meter across.

Palace VI F, with two entrances, attests wooden beams inserted along the interior of the western wall; hollows to receive them are evident. Stone bases for vertical supports also appear on the floor. Because the retaining wall for the structure displays developed masonry employing the offset technique (Fig. 52), Palace VI F has been ascribed to the final phases of Troia VI (ca. 1430-1300 BCE).

Palace VI E is characterized by the remarkably fine finish on the exterior masonry of its eastern wall; it dates to the end of Troia VI (1400-1300 BCE).

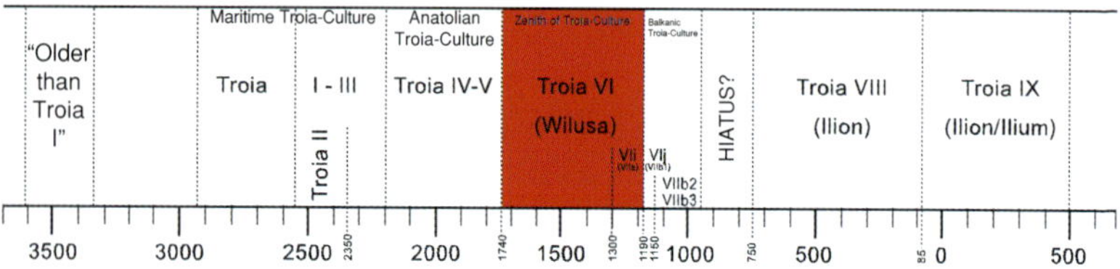

11. (Info Panel 3) The Northeast Bastion – Troia VI

You are now standing on foundations that once supported an altar associated with the Greco-Roman Temple of Athena (see Info Panel 4). The superstructure had fallen prey to stone-robbers even before Schliemann began excavating here in 1871. Other foundations –for statues, dedicatory gifts, altars, and other small monuments– were uncovered at this level contemporary with the Temple, and fragments of marble décor were found scattered throughout the area.

Fig. 72 Reconstruction of Troia VI. © Ch. Haußner.

The Northeast Bastion (Troia VI)

Architecturally the most impressive construction of Late Bronze Age Troia (Figs. 72-75), this bastion belonged to the massive fortifications of Troia VI. It enclosed a 10 m deep artesian well sunk during late Troia VI and revamped in Troia VIi (=VIIa). This source –to which access from the lower settlement was also provided– was sheltered by massive stone foundations 20 x 15 m and at least nine meters in height (today preserved to 7 m) founded upon the bedrock and supporting some sort of sundried mud-brick superstructure.

During Troia VIII/IX, the bastion was incorporated into the temenos wall of the Temple of Athena. Along the north of the tower are remains of a narrow staircase established during Troia VIII to provide access to a source of water (Fig. 73; not visible from your present vantage point). From the east, the wall surrounding the lower city adjoined the citadel here, with a doorway providing access.

Fig. 73 Aerial view of the northeastern bastion of Troia VI. From the north.

Fig. 74
The northeastern bastion (Troia VI) as it appears today. Steps leading downward to a deep well (Troia VIII), and the retaining wall of the Athena Temple precinct (Troia VIII/IX) after restoration.

Fig. 75 Reconstruction of the northeastern bastion of Troia VI. © Ch. Haußner.

The Great Theater in the Background (Troia VIII/IX)

Behind the tower to the east, you see a semicircular depression in the hillside that marks the location of the large theater that served Greek and Roman Ilion (Figs. 76, 77). This theater, richly ornamented with sculpture, welcomed up to 6000 guests. Built in the fourth century BCE, it was destroyed by Fimbria in 85 BCE and eventually restored by the emperor Augustus (31 BCE – 14 CE); it has been only partially excavated.

Fig. 76
The Great Theater following excavation. From the northeast.

Fig. 77 The Great Theater as it must once have appeared: a reconstruction.

12. (Info Panel C) Flora and Fauna

From this elevation above the plain you can see how intensively farmed the present landscape is. This cultivation threatens not only the dense archaeological evidence in the surroundings, but the flora and fauna naturally existing in the ecosystem as well. Homer's *Iliad* includes the names of about 30 various plants, and the archaeobotanic evidence has revealed well beyond 300 species.

Today there are far fewer birds visiting the environs of Troia during migration; for a long time now no cranes at all have been spotted. The sandy banks of the Scamander still offer a haven, however; the hoopoe and the red-capped shrike, as well as the emerald lizard are still in evidence. Varieties of orchids and iris now seldom seen are still surviving here. To preserve what we can both of the natural variety and of the cultural heritage here is a major goal of the national park. Because there is unfortunately still some regression, the new master plan should minimize the loss of irreplaceable "treasures" –natural as well as archeological.

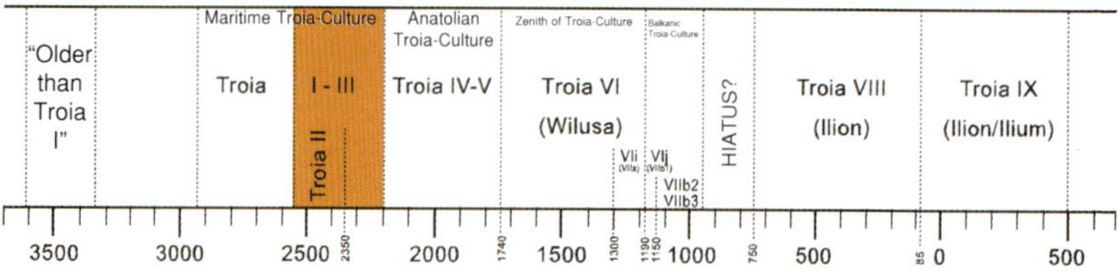

13. (Info Panel 5 a) The Citadel Wall – Troia II/III

From here you have a glimpse of the exterior of the citadel walls of Troia II and III (ca. 2550-2200 BCE), those of the "Burnt City" of Schliemann.

The handmade and fired mudbricks employed in the modern reconstruction serve to protect the original crumbling and severely burnt clay bricks hidden beneath them (Fig. 78) –also preserved to this height (4 m). The heat from the flames had baked the upper and exterior surfaces of the wall to the reddish hue that the reconstruction simulates.

Directly behind and parallel to the fortifications –inside the citadel– lie the remains of a structure known as a

Fig. 78 The burnt mudbricks in the Troia II fortifications as excavated (now preserved beneath the restoration).

Fig. 79 The protective roofing over the megaron of Troia II/III in Quadrat G6.

megaron. When excavated in 1998/99, the mudbrick walls on the stone foundations still stood to a height of more than 1.5 m.

The protective roof built during the summer of 2003 has enabled us to keep this megaron as well as the preserved stretch of fortification wall visible to the public without threat to the original mudbrick masonry. The roof (Fig. 79) not only conveys the more rounded form the mound displayed before excavation, but has even been engineered to reflect the approximate height of Hisarlık as discovered by Schliemann in 1871. The shape, moreover, resembles a billowing sail, recalling the nearly constant northeasterly winds that certainly did waft riches to the site; ancient ships were compelled to bide their time in Beşik Bay awaiting a stray breeze from the southwest that would take them through the straits and onwards towards the Black Sea.

The generous support of ABB AG (Mannheim), DaimlerChrysler AG (Stuttgart), Siemens Sanayi ve Ticaret A.Ş. (Istanbul), and the Friends of Troy have made this protective roofing possible. Björn Rimner designed the project, supervised by Professors Cheret, Knoll, and Sobek from Stuttgart University.

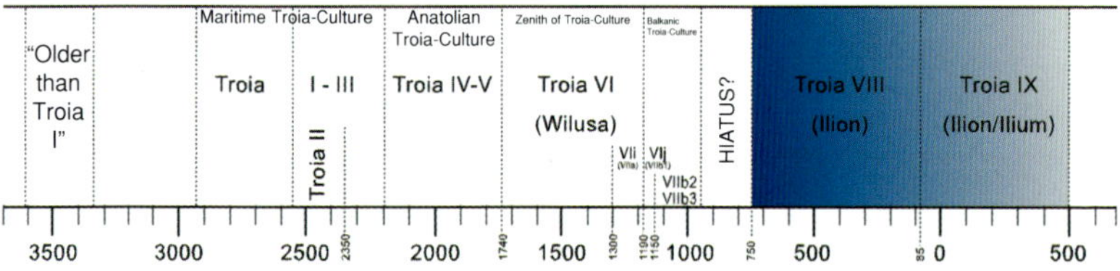

14. (Info Panel 4) The Temple of Athena – Troia VIII/IX

You now stand in what was once the forecourt of the Temple of Athena that stood in the city during the Greek and Roman periods. Looking down into Schliemann and Dörpfeld's trench below, you see various marble architectural members from the Temple of Athena (Figs. 80–84); these have "percolated" downward –during excavation and over the years– from the level at which you now stand.

The temple, which stood on a stylobate 36 x 16 m, was surrounded by a peripteros of Doric columns supporting a coffered ceiling (Fig. 81). Along the entablature above the colonnades ran metopes (a series of sculpted plaques), the best known of which undoubtedly portrays Apollo Helios (now in Berlin; Fig. 18). According to the historian Strabo, construction of the temple had long been accredited to Lysimachus, compatriot and successor of Alexander the Great. Recent investigations by C.B. Rose,

Fig. 80 Reconstruction of Troia VIII. © Ch. Haußner.

Fig. 81 Fragment of the coffered ceiling from the Temple of Athena.

Fig. 82 Fragment of the raking geison from the Temple of Athena.

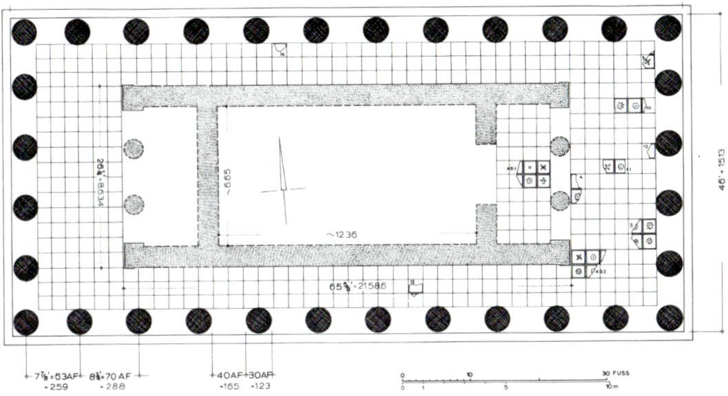

Fig. 83 Reconstructed ground plan of the Temple of Athena (B. Rose).

Fig. 84
The Temple of Athena.
Reconstruction of the colonnade before the entrance.

however, have revealed that the foundation trenches for the structure date no earlier than 240/30 BCE, the period of Antiochus Hierax. Construction seems to have lasted into the first half of the second century BCE, when the Attalids of Pergamon held sway over Troia. The temple was then restored in Roman times, most probably by order of Augustus (31 BCE – 14 CE).

In Greek and Roman times the Temple of Athena served as the focal point of annual celebrations in honor of the Goddess –festivals that included sacrifices and athletic contests.

15. Time for a Break!

Pausing here before the 4500-year old gate of Troia II, should you be offered a drink of pure spring water or a glass of Turkish tea by one of the staff, please accept this as a friendly gesture free of charge (courtesy of the Tusan Hotel in Güzelyalı). Hopefully you'll find it a refreshing pause!

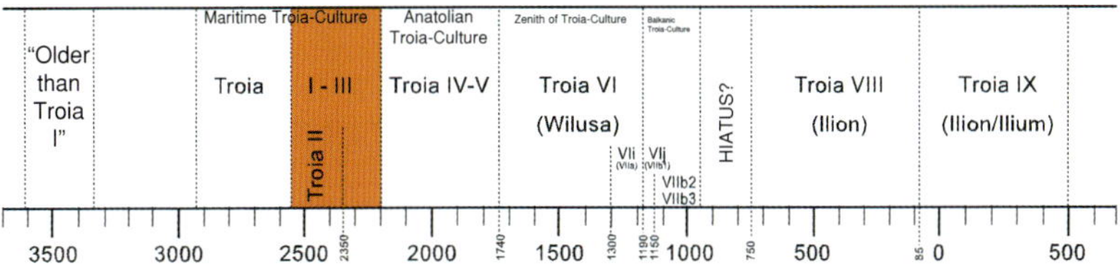

16. (Info Panel 5 b) The Megaron – Troia II/III (ca. 2300-2200 BCE)

The megaron before you (a long narrow structure with a "front porch" enclosed at the sides by extensions of the lateral walls of the structure –a forerunner of the Greek temple plan) of mudbrick masonry upon stone foundations came to light during the excavations of 1998-99. The walls of the structure, built immediately inside the citadel fortifications, were preserved to a height of more than 1.5 m (Figs. 41, 85). C-14 analysis of carbonized grains of barley found inside the building provide a final date for the use of the building (destroyed by fire) between 2290 and 2200 BCE. A central hearth measured 1.2 m in diameter; white plaster covered the interior walls, and the whitewashed floor bore the imprint and charred remnants of reed mats (Figs. 85, 86). The wealth of finds inside indicate at least some cult activity (Fig. 87).

Just to the north of this structure are the remains of still other megara which have only been partly excavated. A shift in the orientation of the complex demonstrates that these structures must be ascribed to a phase transitional between Troia II and III; Gate FO was clearly no longer in use.

Fig. 85
Troia II/II, burnt traces of reed mats on the plastered floor of the megaron in Quadrat G6.

Fig. 86 Virtual reconstruction of the megaron interior (Quadrat G6).

Fig. 87
Ritual vessel with worshippers.
From the megaron in Quadrat G6 (Troia II/III).

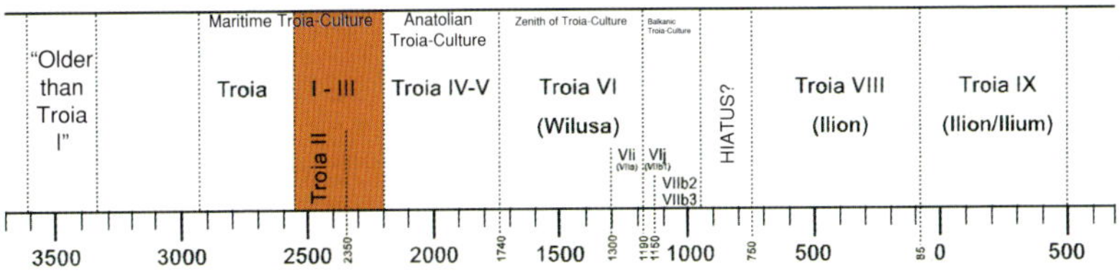

17. (Info Panel 5) The Fortification Wall – Troia I

Here you see a stretch of defense walls dating to the early and middle phases of Troia I, including a tower-like projection behind the southern gate of the period (Figs. 39, 88). The approach was only two meters wide.

The settlement of Troia I was built directly upon the bedrock ca. 2920 BCE. An accumulation of deposit reaching four meters in depth implies a long continuity. The fortifications, which display only a slight inclination, suggest a modest settlement some 90 m in diameter.

In front of the tower there was at least one stele (Fig. 89); the upper part depicts a human figure in relief, possibly armed. The tradition of such stelai survived at Troia

Fig. 88 The South Gate of Troia I. Reconstruction showing the mudbrick superstructure.

Fig. 89
Stone stele with a face in relief.

Fig. 90 Eye motif on a rim sherd from an open bowl (Troia I).

for centuries; at least one millennium later we again see such upright stone blocks outside the South Gate of Troia VI (cf. Info Panel 12).

You will encounter further remains from Troia I (Fig. 90) when you reach Info Panel 7.

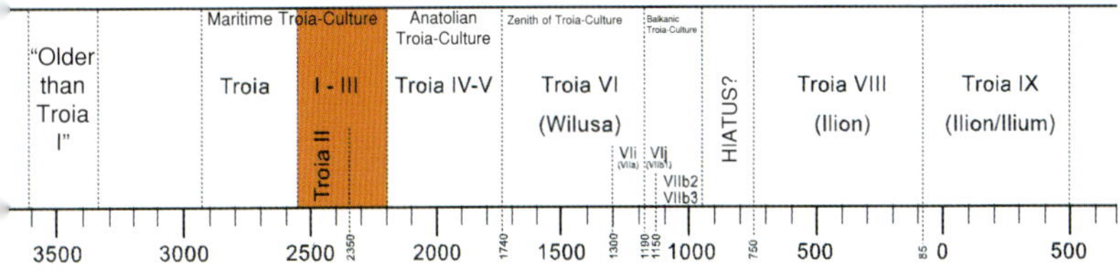

18. (Info Panel 6) The Residence (Manor House) – Troia II

The impressive "parcel" of strata comprising the Trojan Second Settlement on the citadel represents an accumulation of three meters. The excavations here have enabled us to separate the fill into eight building levels, each of which indicates a renovation in the fortifications and/or the structures inside. The most noteworthy periods are those of Troia II c and Troia II g (the latter representing the "Burnt City" in which Schliemann discovered his "Treasure of Priam").

Most of the architectural remains visible today represent Troia II c (Figs. 41, 91). You see a series of three long structures of megaron type. The plan of the largest, Megaron II A (some 30 x 14 m) represents a typical megaron –the possible forerunner of the classical Greek temple. Because the original components have been protected by earth, you see only the approximate outlines; details

Fig. 91 Reconstruction of the Residence (Manor House) of Troia II.

of the architecture are lost from view. The façades were once lined with wooden posts, and most significant is that masonry of rectangular stone blocks was employed as an architectural "first" in this region –particularly impressive when we consider that iron tools would not be in use here for over another thousand years!

The main entrance to this complex was the processional Gate FO opposite; behind you, you see the large threshold block (3 x 1.1 m) remaining from a smaller gateway (Gate II C), and there was still another entrance in the west (see Info Panel 8).

The entire citadel of Troia II c thus displays a highly prestigious character (Fig. 91). Here we have a manor house or palace complex that most likely served cult purposes as well. Below the citadel lay a fortified settlement first discovered in the recent campaigns (Figs. 44, 45). Troia II therefore intimates the existence of an "upper" class in both senses of the word. It was most likely a privileged class that inhabited the acropolis, while in the lower city lived the simpler local (?) folk probably surviving from the late or end-phases of Troia I.

The preeminent character of the upper city is reflected in the finds as well. The so-called treasures demonstrate a luxury not only awesome for its time, but astonishing in its workmanship as well. Troia counts as one of the earliest

Fig. 92 A typical bowl of early pottery made on the potter's wheel.

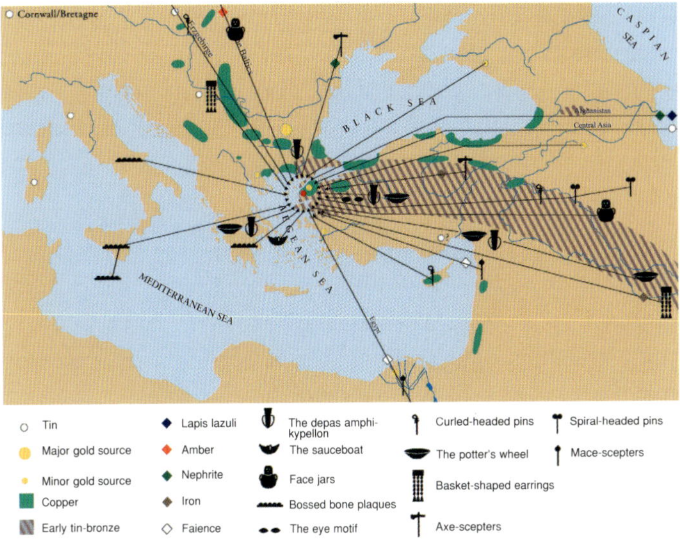

Fig. 93 Various Trojan contacts proposed over the past 120 years: raw materials and cultural parallels. Today we recognize that not all represent concrete evidence of direct connections.

prehistoric sites known to have employed tin as an alloy in the production of bronze, and is also known as the earliest site within the Aegean realm to have employed the potter's wheel (not to forget the rectangular hewn blocks in the stone masonry!). Materials such as tin and semiprecious stones such as lapis lazuli and carnelian must have been imported from afar, implying extended trade relations that also underline the importance of the site in the Early Bronze Age (Figs. 92, 93).

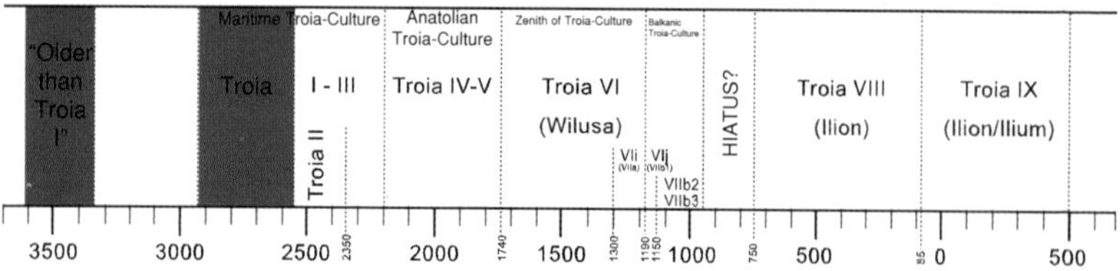

19. (Info Panel 7) Schliemann's Trench – Troia I

During the first three years of his campaign, Schliemann chose to work in a 40-m wide trench laid out N-S across the middle of the mound (Figs. 94-96). This was a sondage 17 meters in depth (opened clear to the bedrock), an attempt to find the "City of Priam." The project resulted in the partial or total destruction of significant architectural structures belonging to the levels above, but at the base of the trench Schliemann laid bare the walls from the early period of Troia I (ca. 2920 BCE) that you see from here.

It was first during the American excavations of the 1930s, however, and then again in the campaigns since 1988 that the period of Troia I was investigated in detail.

Just below you lie remnants of a slanting wall supported by stone fill; this has been interpreted as part of the rampart-like fortifications belonging to the early Troia I period.

Fig. 94 Wall "g" of Troia I with its herringbone masonry as it appeared in the Schliemann-Trench in 1893. From the Dörpfeld Archives at the German Archaeological Institute in Athens (no. 327).

Fig. 95
The Schliemann Trench
in 1989.

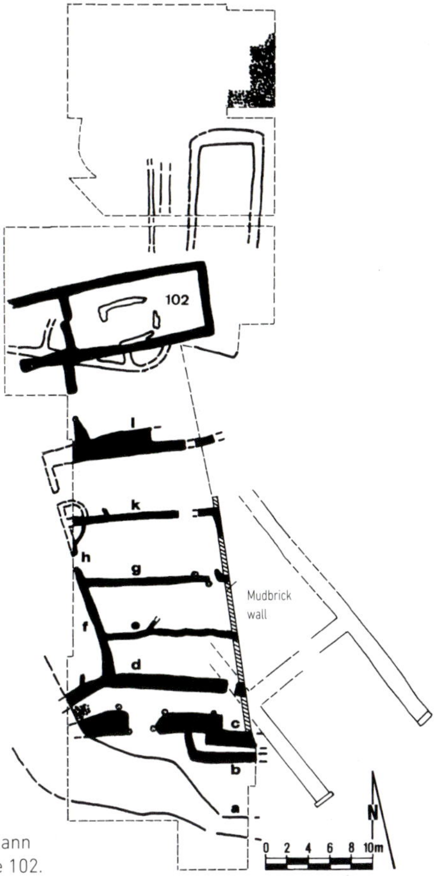

Fig. 96
Plan from the Schliemann
Trench showing House 102.

The parallel lines of fieldstone you see beyond the rampart represent foundations of relatively spacious "long-houses" of the Early Bronze Age (ca. 2920 BCE). Some of these houses, laid out side by side, display internal divisions separating front and back rooms. Of particular interest is the herringbone masonry (in which alternating stone courses are set in opposing diagonals) a fine example of which is Wall "g" (Fig. 94). Outstanding among these structures is House 102 from Level I b, which in both form and size suggests a megaron (Fig. 96). The superstructures of these houses were presumably of sun-dried mudbrick –or possibly of wooden posts and wattle-and-daub. The roofs –of which nothing remained– would have been flat and covered with mud.

The long terrace-wall built in 1988 to protect the scarp was therefore appropriately constructed entirely of sun-dried mudbricks. It runs along a line approximating the position of the rear walls of the "long-houses."

In the north of the great trench appeared several child burials with skeletons found in the fetal position. In this period it was not at all uncommon to bury children within the settlement.

20. (Info Panel D) Troia: the Various Levels

An excellent insight into the strata of the mound of Hisarlık is given by the eastern profile visible southward from where you now stand (cf. Fig. 35). You are now situated atop the citadel fortifications of Troia II, the foundations of which reach to bedrock. Before you lies the "Middle Trench" of Schliemann, opened in 1872. Further work by W. Dörpfeld (1893) and M. Korfmann (1990-96) has resulted in exposing a clear profile with a complete sequence of the strata from Troia II through Troia IX, representing a time span from the mid-third millennium BCE through Roman imperial times.

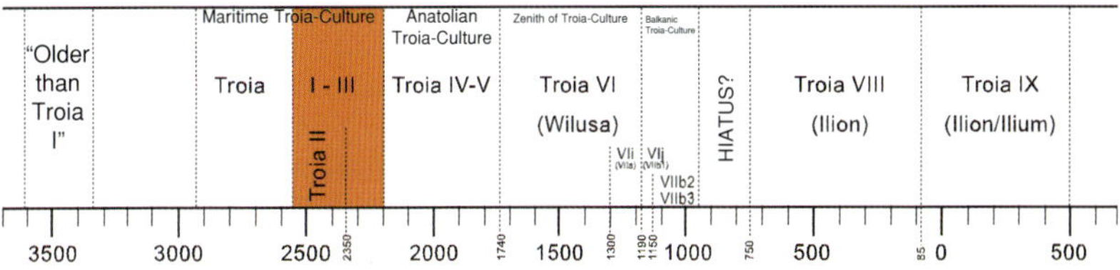

21. (Info Panel 8) The Ramp – Troia II

From here you look out over the defense walls of the Troia II citadel and its famed –and now partially restored– ramp (Figs. 41-43, 97, 98).

The settlement of Troia II was built upon the remains of Troia I a – Troia I e (= Middle Troia I). This Trojan Second Settlement has been subdivided into eight building phases: Troia II a through Troia II h.

Within this period the defenses surrounding the citadel were enlarged several times, widening the area of the upper city. Such renovation is often apparent in the walling-up of earlier gates.

The four-meter broad wall –330 m long in the latest phase visible here– was of mudbrick masonry built upon the limestone foundations before you. It enclosed an area of some 9,000 m^2. This impressive paved ramp –originally protected by high mudbrick walls– led upwards to the entrance visible above, Gate FM.

Fig. 97
The citadel fortifications of Troia II with the ramp leading to Gate FM, a photo from 1890. Dörpfeld Archives of the German Archaeological Institute in Athens (no. 321).

Judging from its grandeur and orientation, the eastern entrance complex (Gate FO; see Info Panel 6 and Fig. 41) must have served as the main gateway; the appreciable slope approaching it too must have been bridged by such a ramp. The catastrophic fire that destroyed the citadel of Troia II left a two-meter-deep layer of ashen remains.

To your left you see a street leading to an earlier gate of Troia II. It was above this and to the right –where a small fig tree is now growing from the wall– that Schliemann discovered the legendary "Treasure of Priam" (Fig. 99). It had been deposited, as we know today, within the tower of an earlier gateway razed during the construction of the ramp. Because of these rich finds in a burnt layer accompanied by this impressive ramped entrance (Schliemann's "Scaean Gate"), the excavator at first selected the city of Troia II as the most likely candidate for the object of his search – the Ilion of Homer. In this, he missed his mark by some 1,250 years. In 1890, however, the year he

Fig. 98 Reconstruction of the ramp and Gate FM. © Ch. Haußner.

Fig. 99 Treasure A, the "Treasure of Priam".

died, Schliemann conceded his error. More than twenty "Treasures of Troia" recovered by Schliemann at Troia were dispersed among nine different locations in seven cities throughout the world, many of which –since World War II– have been housed in Moscow and St. Petersburg.

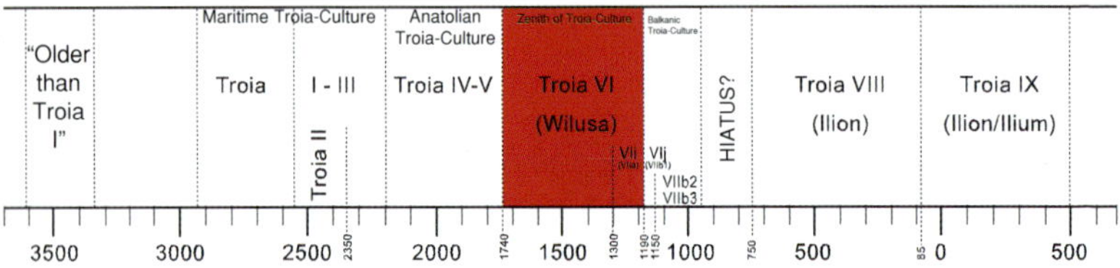

22. (Info Panel 9) The Palatial Residence (VI M) – Troia VI

You are now on the southern rim of the citadel of Troia VI, directly above the massive fortifications of the period. You should picture the slope of the wall you see –exposed here only at the crown– extending another five meters outward as it descends (as can be seen in the east, cf. Info Panel 2).

Inside the ring-wall to the north (on your left) stands the impressive 27-meter-long retaining wall of House VI M, sloping slightly inward. The structure stood on the lowermost terrace of the citadel of Troia VI, beyond any doubt a part of the palatial complex here (Figs. 100, 101). The ceramics of this period display not only highly developed local manufacture, but a penchant for Mycenaean imports as well (Figs. 102, 103).

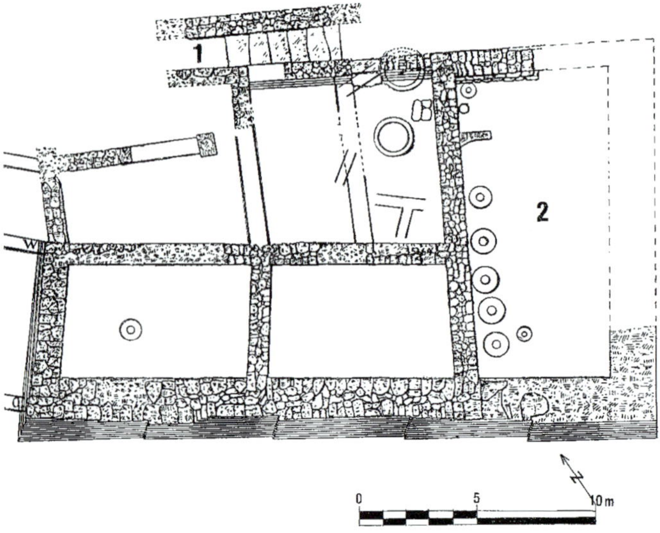

Fig. 100 The ground plan of House VI M, with (1) marking the stairway leading upward-probably to a second story-and (2), the room with large pithoi for storage.

Fig. 101 Reconstruction of House VI M. © Ch. Haußner.

Fig. 102 Sherds of Mycenaean pottery from Troia VI.

The four "saw-tooth" offsets on the exterior immediately strike the eye (Fig. 52) –as well as a slight curvature (undulation) in the masonry; to achieve this, the blocks had to be carefully hewn. These details, more than stylistic, appear in other contemporary masonry at the site as well (cf. Info Panel 2). On the one hand these details may speak for the cultivated taste and status of the palace residents, but on the other hand they must have been functional as well, the offsets probably useful in supporting the timber-frame and mudbrick superstructure. Undulation would have been a precaution against seismic shocks. The carefully worked blocks fit together precisely without any mortar, as is best seen in the lower and less weathered courses of these stone walls. We can appreciate this achievement even more if we recall that no iron implements were yet available in this period. Homer sang again and again of the "beautiful" walls of Ilios.

A broad avenue ran between House VI M and the citadel wall. Further along the continuation of this street you see remains uncovered in more recent excavation.

Within the 'L'-shaped palace House VI M there were several rooms, the purposes of which little is known. Large vessels (pithoi) that have survived do suggest the storage of some provisions. Of a second story, evidenced by the few

Fig. 103 Arrowheads of bronze and bone (Troia VI and VIIa).

surviving steps of a staircase, nothing remains. The shorter sides of this residence, like those of other structures from Troia VI, seem to be radially oriented toward the center of the citadel, implying a uniformly planned layout with wide streets between the buildings.

During the subsequent period, Troia VI i (=Troia VII a), House VI M was renovated and continued in use. Smaller houses were now built up immediately inside the defense wall, some of which you can make out behind you to the west. Troia VI i (ca. 1300-1180 BCE) –together with the preceding late phases of Troia VI– represents the golden age of Troia/Wilusa.

Aerial view of Troy.

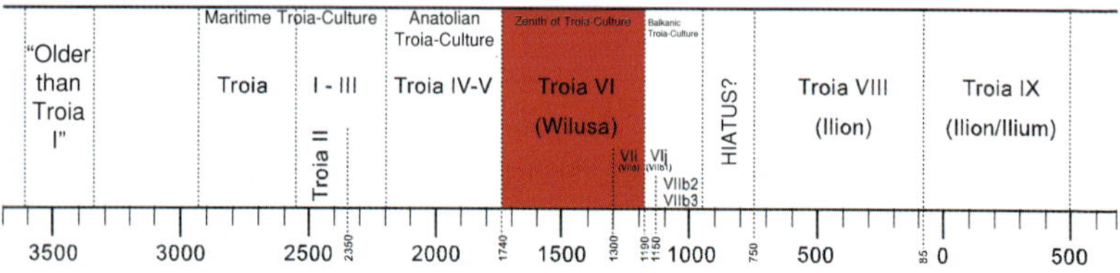

23. (Info Panel 10) The Sanctuary – Troia VI-IX

As we know from both the ancient sources and the excavations, although Troia was "the sacred Ilios" even as early as Homer's age, it was most particularly in Greek and Roman times that the site was renowned as a religious center.

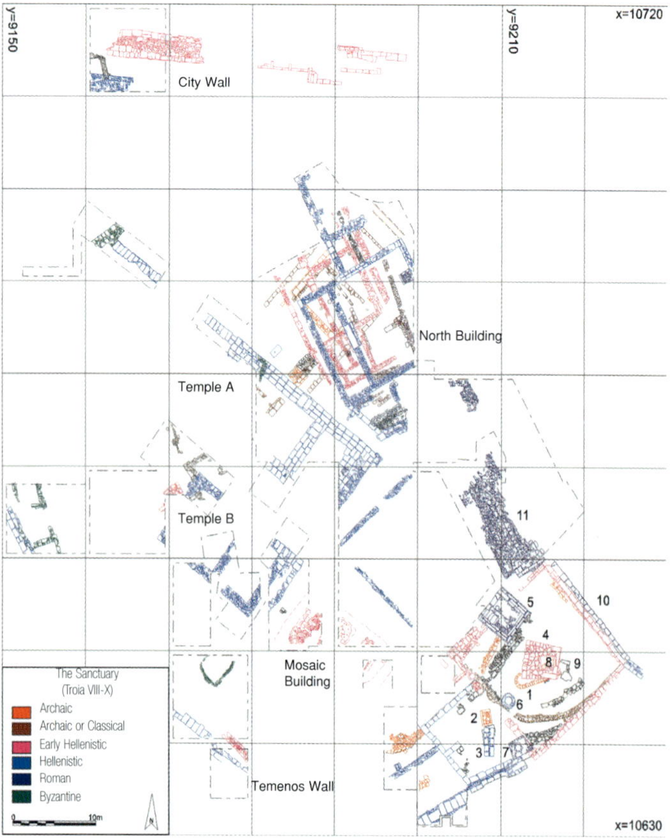

Fig. 104 Plan of the structures surviving in the Sanctuary (Troia VIII-X).

The religious precinct before you was first constructed perhaps as early as 700 BCE. Its foundations cut into the remnants of the lower cities of Troia VI and VII that had covered the area here. Enclosed by a wall (Figs. 104, 105), the Sanctuary continued in use throughout the Hellenistic period and well into imperial Roman times –needless to say, repeatedly elevated and revamped; the course of the enclosure wall was altered several times. In early levels, an altar of limestone stood near the center of the sanctuary, with one semicircular end (No. 1) protruding from beneath a more recent altar (No. 4) and a sacrificial pit (No. 8). Lower on the slope, you see two more altars, one (No. 2) from the archaic period and the other (No. 3) from Hellenistic times. Visible today are also sacrificial pits (Nos. 8, 9) and wells (Nos. 6, 7). The northeastern wall of the upper sanctuary (No. 10), neatly constructed

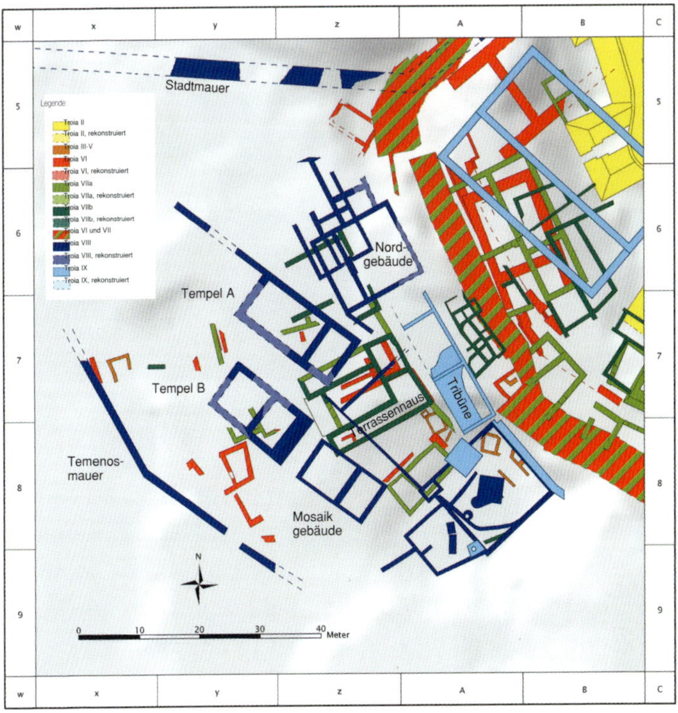

Fig. 105 Phase-plan of the structures outside the citadel to the west (Troia V-X).

Fig. 106 Hellenistic terracottas.

of rectangular blocks, rises in front of the Troia VI fortifications. This dates to Hellenistic times. In the late fourth century BCE both parts of the sacred precinct seem to have been reorganized –very possibly the consequence of Alexander the Great's visit to Ilion in 334 BCE.

The precinct suffered greatly when Fimbria sacked Ilion in 85 BCE. Within the framework of a later and

Fig. 107 Clay plaque depicting a figure on horseback.

more elevated sanctuary probably established by Emperor Augustus (31 BCE – 14 CE), a new altar (No. 5) was erected, near which you also see the foundations of a stepped podium (No. 11) –most likely a grandstand for the religious ceremonies performed here.

To which deities the Sanctuary may have been dedicated remains in question. The many terracotta statuettes of Cybele, Demeter, and an equestrian –Dardanus(?)– found at Troia (Figs. 106, 107) give us at least a clue.

Further off appear trenches from the recent campaigns. Here we have exposed more of the sanctuary (two temples) as well as a stratified sequence for the lower cities of Troia VI and VII. The strata here –particularly significant for the 14th to 12th centuries BCE (Late Troia VI, VI i [= VII a], and VII b)– had been partially preserved due to the overlying remains of the religious structures.

24. (Info Panel 10 a) The Lower City of (W)Ilios/Wilusa – Late Troia VI

Before you lies the lower city of Late Troia VI and Troia VI i (14th-13th cent. BCE) located outside the citadel walls to the west. Clearly visible are the sturdy stone foundations of the densely packed houses that lined a stone-paved approach to the citadel (Figs. 105, 108-110).

Particularly of note is the nearly complete outline of the Terrace House from Troia VI i, the back rooms of which supported a second story and may have served cult purposes, judging from a bronze statuette (Fig. 111) and the ceramic image of a bull found here.

Following the earthquake that marked the end of Troia VI, the citadel Gate VI U was closed off and the course of the streets altered. Troia VII a (= VI i) was then destroyed in battle, as evidenced by the number of weapons, burnt remains, and skeletons found. In Period VII b, when immigrants from the Balkans settled at Troia, settlement

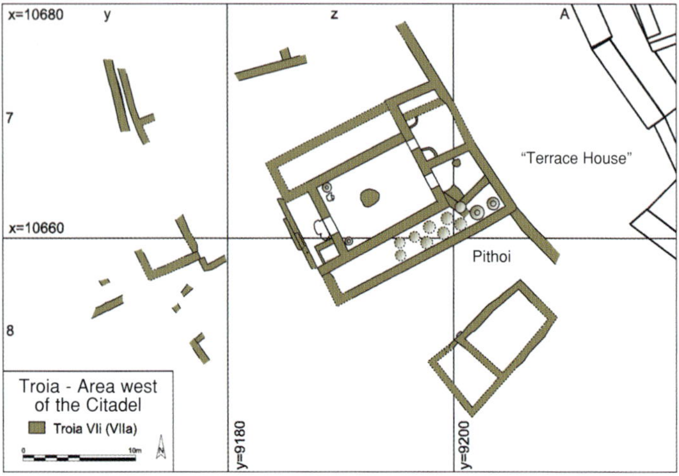

Fig. 108 Ground plan of the Terrace House (Troia VI i = VII a).

Fig. 109 Aerial photograph of the western lower city (Troia V-X).

Fig. 110
Reconstruction of the Terrace House.

Fig. 111
A bronze statuette from the Terrace House.

was restricted to the citadel and the immediate environs. So dense was the settlement that even the earlier streets and squares were overrun, congested with houses and outbuildings, filled –as you can see– with large storage vessels (pithoi).

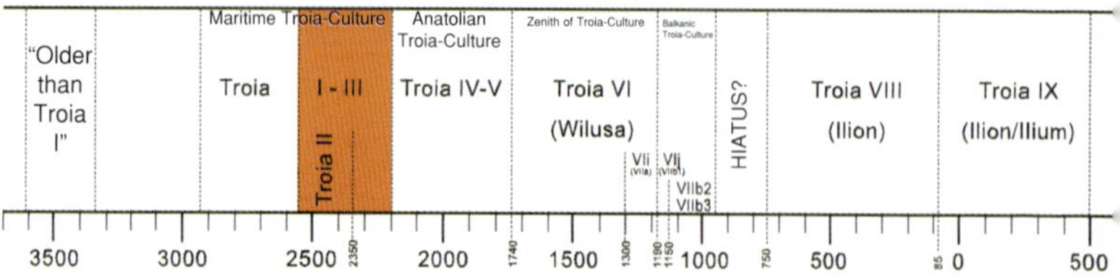

25. (Info Panel 10 b) The Water Cave of Troia/Wilusa (KASKAL.KUR) – Troia II-IX

In the southwest of the lower city, an artificial water-cave with underground tunnels totaling ca. 160 m in length (three arms supplying water from a subterranean source) was excavated during the seasons of 1997 through 2001 (Figs. 112-114). Evaluated by the ^{230}uranium/thorium method, the sinter deposited in some of the galleries cut into siliceous bedrock dates as early as the third millennium BCE.

This water-cave, which had been serving Troia for a good one thousand years by the period of Troia VI (second millennium BCE), may therefore be identified with the "subterranean passageway" of the god KASKAL.KUR,

Fig. 112 Aerial photograph showing the position of the shafts of the water-cave.

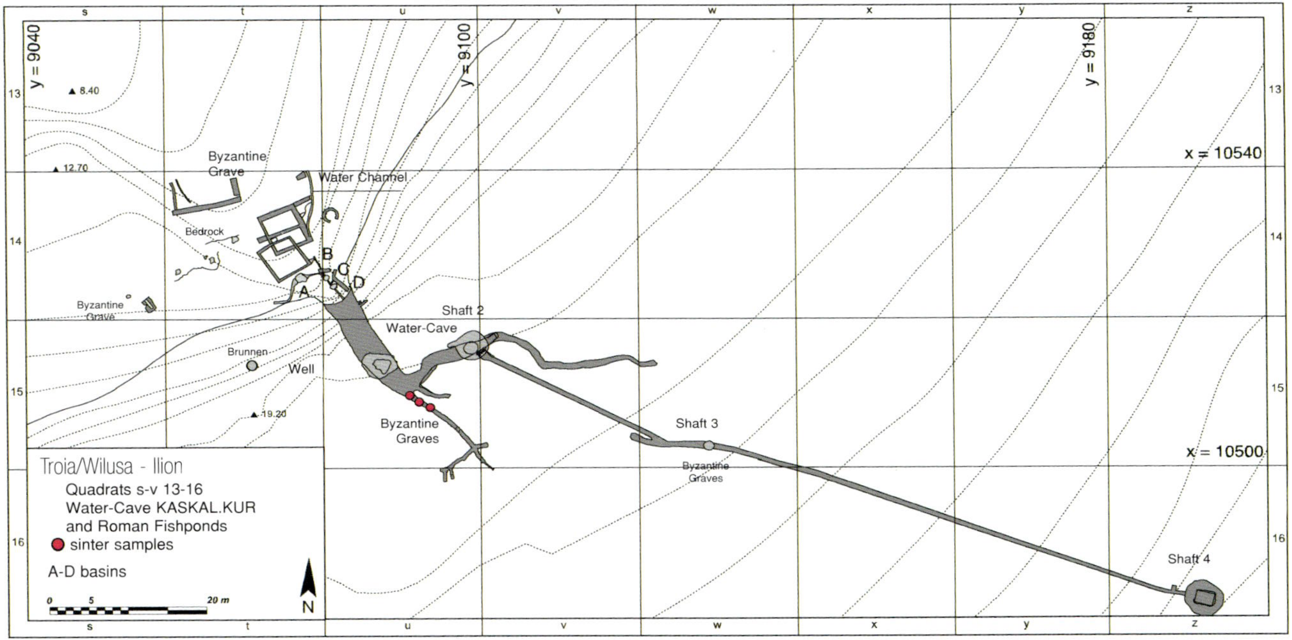

Fig. 113 Plan of the water-cave.

Fig. 114 The northern gallery of the water-cave.

closely associated with water. It was around 1280 BCE that KASKAL.KUR was called upon as Trojan witness to a treaty sworn between the Hittite monarch Muwatalli II and King Alaksandu of Wilusa (= [W]ilios); thus we have evidence for a second deity –in addition to Appaliuna (= Apollo ?)– vouching on behalf of Troia.

The gallery system runs through the bedrock to the east, connecting with four shafts at depths up to 17 m below the surface.

A protective wall narrowing the entrance to the galleries marks the smaller extent of the prehistoric water-cave, from which water was distributed to several rock-cut basins (A–D). In the Roman period (2nd – 3rd cent. CE), clay pipes directed the flow into "fishponds" outside the water-cave, and in Byzantine times (12th – 13th cent. CE) there was most likely a garden here; water ran through channels lined with stone.

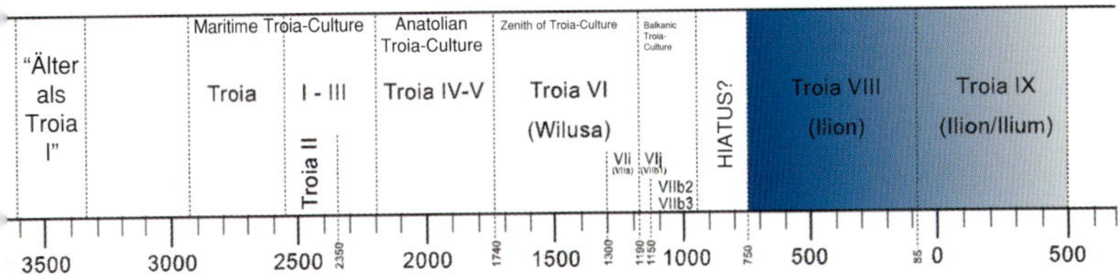

26. (Info Panel 11) The Odeion and Bouleuterion – Troia IX

The Odeion

Before you is the Roman Odeion, a small amphitheater where concerts, lectures and other events took place (Fig. 115); beyond it you see the fortification wall of Troia VI and the single column surviving from the large "Pillar-House" of the same period. Behind you stand the partially excavated remains of baths from Roman Imperial times. The baths, the Odeion, and the nearby Bouleuterion all lay on the fringes of the agora (marketplace), the central stage of public life. The semicircular *orchestra* of the odeion was backed by a *skene* (stage building) that included an over life-sized representation of the emperor Hadrian (117–138 CE, Fig. 60). Facing the stage, behind an arc of vertical plaques, rose tiers of seats fashioned from limestone blocks and accessed by radial aisles.

Fig. 115 Aerial view of the Odeion after restoration. From the south.

A sculpted head of Augustus found here (Fig. 116) suggests that the Odeion may have been erected in honor of his visit in 20 BCE –and that perhaps upon this visit he might first have heard a reading of Virgil's ***Aeneid*** (in praise of his forefathers), a masterpiece the poet left unfinished at his death in 19 BCE. In the area were found many architectural members as well, including terracotta décor that reflect the ornament of the roof (Fig. 117).

The Bouleuterion

Some 70 m to your right, you see the Bouleuterion, the city assembly hall of Greek Ilion and Roman Ilium; part of the structure overlies the citadel wall of Troia VI. The inner chamber was completely walled off so that the council could conduct business in private.

Fig. 116
Sculpted head of Augustus from the Odeion.

Fig. 117 Ornamented roof tiles found near the Odeion.

Historical Outline of the Greek and Roman Ilion/Ilium

Most scholars today agree that Greek colonists established a settlement on the mound of Hisarlık around 700 BCE (Troia VIII), a date roughly corresponding to the *Iliad* (= Homer). The fame of Ilion's legendary past became great enough to draw powerful political leaders such as the Persian King Xerxes (480 BCE) and Alexander the Great of Macedon (334 BCE) to the site, where they offered sacrifices to the city's patron goddess Athena as well as to the Homeric heroes. Upon occasion such visits triggered comprehensive architectural improvements –secular as well as sacred.

The lower city was laid out in rectangular blocks, or insulae.

In 85 BCE the site was destroyed by the disloyal Roman general Fimbria, but nevertheless managed to survive into imperial times (Troia IX) thanks to the

Roman emperors –Augustus in particular, who brought the city to a new floruit. Members of the imperial family, who often visited the city, widened the cultural spectrum as witnessed by impressive works of architecture (Figs. 59, 76, 83) such as the Great Theater, the Bouleuterion, and the Temple of Athena.

The Romans exhibited a particular fondness for Troia, for they could trace their imperial lineage back to the Trojan hero Aeneas. In the post-Homeric legends, Aeneas not only survives the war but takes refuge in Italy, thus representing a forefather from Ilion (a site that consequently became the "mother-city" of Rome). Various coins were minted representing the flight of Aeneas and his family (Fig. 19); these emphasize the Romans' regard for this legendary past, most pronounced during the Julian and Claudian dynasties.

Fig. 118 Reconstruction of the South Gate (Troia VI). © Ch. Haußner.

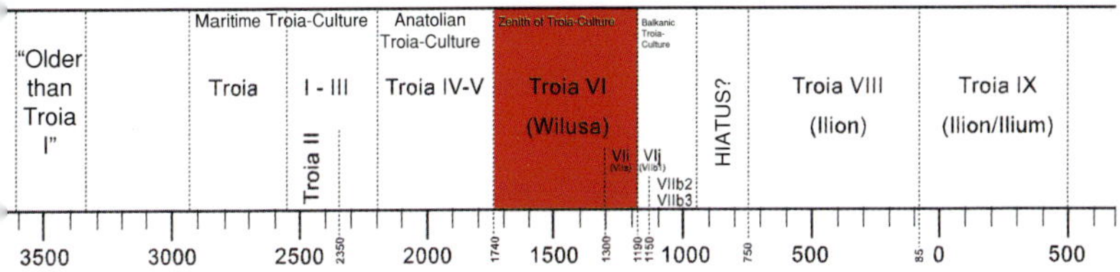

27. (Info Panel 12) The South Gate – Troia VI

You now stand just before the southern entranceway to the citadel of Troia VI, which must have been the main gate in this period (Fig. 118). Today, however, all that you can make out is the stone-flagged approach leading up toward the citadel. A novelty of the flourishing times of Troia VI i (= VII a) is the drain running down the center of the road under the pavement slabs.

The South Tower

This tower (10 x 9.5 m) in the south was added to the citadel fortifications during Troia VI i (= VII a), i.e. in the 13th century BCE. The walls, constructed directly upon bedrock and now preserved to a height of ca. two meters, stylistically resemble those of the contemporary East Tower. Immediately before the South Tower you see several stelai, a typical witness to the importance of portals in ancient Anatolian cult –probably to be associated with Apollo (Appaliuna ?).

The "Pillar-House"

To your left behind the South Tower you see a lone remaining pillar marking the location of the "Pillar-House," so-named for the two pillars in the central hall, which certainly supported a sturdy roof if not a second story. With a ground plan of 27 x 12.5 m, this represents one of the largest houses in Troia VI.

The Finds

Among the most frequently recovered finds characterizing Period VI is the pottery known as "Anatolian Gray Ware," so named to reflect its distribution (Fig. 119). Vessels of this ware were often ornamented with series of wavy incised lines. Most important are the Mycenean imports, which testify to economic contact between the Anatolian city and trade center of Troia and the great Aegean power of Mycenae –thus underlining the significance of long-distance trade.

Fig. 119 A typical bowl of Anatolian Gray Ware (Troia VI).

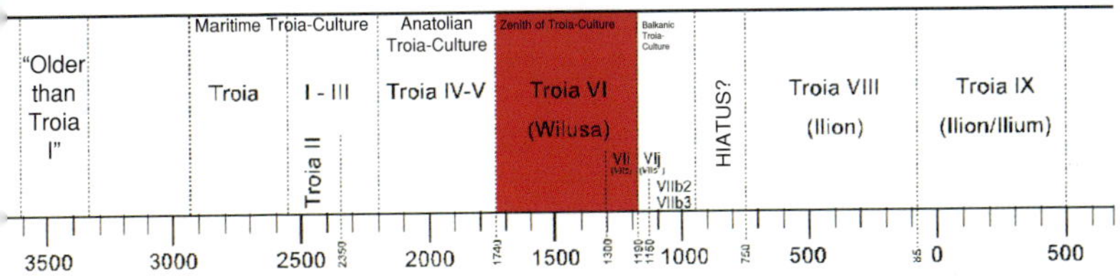

28. The Lower City – Troia VI-IX

By now you have a general understanding of the most significant aspects of the more than three millennia of cultural development at Troia reflected in the citadel remains exposed over 32 excavation campaigns. On the one hand we have the responsibility of preserving these monuments and making them accessible to visitors, while on the other hand excavation must continue. The work in progress you can see for yourself, "live" and from remarkably close range if you visit during the summer months, an experience possible at very few sites today. At present this opportunity applies only to the citadel itself, even though there is also much of note beyond the walls of Ilion, where excavation is also in progress. Here we wish to offer you a summary of findings from the lower city (Figs. 54, 59, 61, 62, 120, 121) at present not open to visitors. For this we apologize and thank you for your patience and cooperation.

While excavation at Troia prior to 1988 was restricted primarily to the citadel, the new multifaceted investigations have facilitated progress in areas outside the citadel walls. Since 1993, the Deutsche Forschungsgemeinschaft has been supporting such efforts.

It was, of course, the topography that offered the first clues of where to begin. Logically, where would the inhabitants have expanded outside the citadel, and how far might they have expanded the settlement? Surface survey of the surrounding fields then provided us with a relative distribution of finds –mostly pottery– indicating which areas were more densely settled. Surprising was the number of Bronze Age sherds: how might these have percolated upward through centuries of Greek and Roman dcposit?

Fig. 120 Aerial view of excavations in the lower city. From the south. Photo: H. Öge

Each time the foundations for a new structure were sunk to the bedrock two to three meters below present ground level –a provision given particular consideration in Roman times– some underlying remnants of the past were thrown up to the surface. This process of elevating the prehistoric remains continued throughout the some 800 years

of unbroken Greek and Roman settlement. Think of the countless pits dug into the earth for storage and waste, not to mention foundation trenches and the constant upkeep of water pipes laid beneath the surface; the earlier pottery was splintered into more even smaller sherds. Significant, however, is that these fragments did reach the surface, giving the archaeologist an important preview of what to expect before excavation actually began. When excavated, pre-tested areas did indeed expose such earlier levels, including those of the Late Bronze Age (Troia VI and VIi [= VIIa]). Thus at one place we discovered the remains of a very impressive wooden bulwark dating back to what must have represented an outlying district of the "Maritime Troia Culture" of Troia I-III (Figs. 44, 45, 121).

Excavation is not necessarily the second step, however. Modern geophysical prospection now offers an economically feasible method to comb large undisturbed areas for ancient structures now buried beneath the surface (Fig. 59). Subsequent excavation can thus be much more accurately and efficiently focused. Archeomagnetic survey has succeeded in producing a plan of structures laid out in rectangular city blocks (*insulae* or islands) covering much of

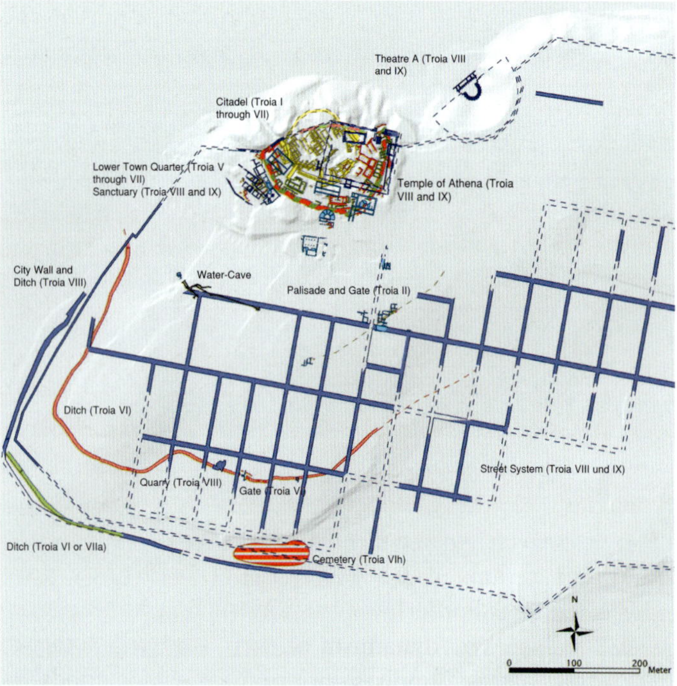

Fig. 121 Traces of settlement (Troia II-IX) in the lower city.

the lower cities of Hellenistic and Roman times (Troia VIII and IX). At least four hundred meters of the Hellenistic fortifications in the west has been accurately mapped out.

The long-predicted existence of a lower settlement during the Late Bronze Age (late Troia VI and Troia VIi [= VIIa]) has finally been verified, along with its exact boundary to the south and west (indicated by the white arrows in Fig. 59). The latter consisted of a protective ditch cut into the bedrock, 1.5-2 m deep and more than three meters across, 'U'-shaped in section. Apparently in the 13th century (Troia VI i) this barrier was then further extended to the south (Fig. 54). Outside the earlier ditch lay a cemetery dating to Late Troia VI (Fig. 121). Systematic survey begun in the summer of 2002 now also suggests an eastern boundary determined by a sharp drop in Late Bronze Age finds further eastward. At the north, the lower city was limited by the citadel exposed in the excavations of Schliemann and Dörpfeld, so that at present the limits of the lower city of Wilusa are quite well defined.

The state of research at the end of the 2003 campaign suggests that the Trojan city at the end of the second millennium covered an area easily greater than 300,000 m^2, making the settlement fifteen times greater than earlier postulated. With its crowning citadel, the ruins of the city must have presented a grand stage for Homer and his "eye-witnesses" around 700 BCE when the ***Iliad*** was composed. With some 7000 residents, Troia clearly figured as one of the larger cities in this realm; the layout and architecture confirm that it represented a palatial and commercial center in contact with others of this ilk throughout the landscape of Asia Minor and the Near East. If not totally comparable in all aspects to the most important capitals of its day and age, Troia had the great advantage of its borderline situation; such peripheral cities tended to display a dynamism of their own, in contact as they were with the impulses –not to mention the goods– of the world "beyond." Here within the "copper belt" that stretched from the Balkans across northern Anatolia (Fig. 93), metal was probably the most important commodity: not only copper, but gold and tin as well.

As a prehistoric culture, that of Troia (with access to two seas and two continents) played an outstanding role in the second half of the second millennium BCE (most particularly in the 13th and early 12th century, where we can best pinpoint the legendary "Trojan War" (Troia VII a =VI i). In this age the Trojan acropolis –in both size and architectural development– remains unparalled by any settlement north of Greece and the Dardanelles; nor does it meet its match in northern coastal Anatolia. We can really appreciate Troia only when we consider its status as a final outpost dispersing the more advanced civilizations of the Orient to the "barbarians".

Select Bibliography

1. Excavation reports from 1871 to the present

HEINRICH SCHLIEMANN, Trojanische Alterthümer, a report on the excavations at Troia (Leipzig 1874) with the Atlas Trojanischer Alterthümer, photographs complementary to the text (Leipzig 1874)

HEINRICH SCHLIEMANN, Troy and its Remains: A Narrative of Researches and Discoveries Made on the Site of Ilium and in the Trojan Plain. Ed. Philip Smith, transl. Dora Schmitz (London/New York 1875)

HEINRICH SCHLIEMANN, Bericht über die Ausgrabungen in Troja in den Jahren 1871 bis 1873 (Munich/Zurich 1990), with a foreword by Manfred Korfmann and 70 figures as well as 48 plates from the Atlas trojanischer Alterthümer (Munich/Zurich 1990)

HEINRICH SCHLIEMANN, Ilios, Stadt und Land der Trojaner: Forschungen und Entdeckungen in der Troas und besonders auf der Baustelle von Troja (Leipzig 1881)

HEINRICH SCHLIEMANN, Ilios, The City and Country of the Trojans, English translation of the above (London/New York 1881)

HEINRICH SCHLIEMANN, Troia: Ergebnisse meiner neuesten Ausgrabungen auf der Baustelle von Troja, in den Heldengräbern, Bunarbarbaschi und andern Orten der Troas im Jahre 1882 (Leipzig 1884, reprinted by Rainer Gerlach, Dortmund 1984/1987)

HEINRICH SCHLIEMANN, Troja: Results of the Latest Researches and Discoveries on the Site of Homer's Troy, 1882, English translation of the above (London/New York 1884)

HEINRICH SCHLIEMANN, Bericht über die Ausgrabungen in Troja im Jahre 1890 (Leipzig 1891)

WILHELM DÖRPFELD, Troia 1893, Bericht über die im Jahre 1893 in Troia veranstalteten Ausgrabungen (Leipzig 1894)

WILHELM DÖRPFELD, Troja und Ilion: Ergebnisse der Ausgrabungen in den vorhistorischen und historischen Schichten von Ilion 1870-1894 (Athens 1902, reprinted in Osnabrück 1968).

CARL W. BLEGEN, JOHN L. CASKEY, MARION RAWSON, JEROME SPERLING, Troy I: General Introduction. The First and Second Settlements (Princeton 1950)

CARL W. BLEGEN, JOHN L. CASKEY, MARION RAWSON, Troy II: The Third, Fourth and Fifth Settlements (Princeton 1951)

CARL W. BLEGEN, JOHN L. CASKEY, MARION RAWSON, Troy III: The Sixth Settlement (Princeton 1953)

CARL W. BLEGEN, CEDRIC G. BOULTER, JOHN L. CASKEY, MARION RAWSON, Troy IV: Settlements VIIa, VIIb and VIII (Princeton 1958)

CARL W. BLEGEN, Troy and the Trojans (London 1963)

J. LAWRENCE ANGEL, Troy: The Human Remains, Supplementary Monograph 1 (Princeton 1951).

ALFRED R. BELLINGER, Troy: The Coins, Supplementary Monograph 2 (Princeton 1961)

DOROTHY BURR THOMPSON, Troy: The Terracotta Figurines, Supplementary Monograph 3 (Princeton 1963)

GEORGE RAPP Jr., JOHN A. GIFFORD, Troy: The Archaeological Geology, Supplementary Monograph 4 (Princeton 1982)

FRIEDRICH WILHELM GOETHERT, HANS SCHLEIF, Der Athena-Tempel von Ilion (Berlin 1962)

Since 1988 annual excavation reports have appeared regularly in the following periodicals:

* KAZI SONUÇLARI TOPLANTISI, a publication of annual excavation reports (Ankara), in Turkish

* STUDIA TROICA, the Annual of the Troia Project (Mainz), in German and English

* MONOGRAPHS OF STUDIA TROICA, final reports in German or English (Mainz)

2. The landscape and surroundings

JOHN M. COOK, The Troad: An Archaeological and Topographical Study (Oxford University Press 1973)

JOHN V. LUCE, Celebrating Homer's Landscapes (Yale University Press, New Haven - London 1998)

MANFRED KORFMANN, "Troia - A Residential and Trading City at the Dardanelles," in Politeia: Society and State in the Aegean Bronze Age, Proceedings of the Fifth International Conference, Heidelberg 1994, Aegaeum 12, (Liège 1995)

3. Further reading, including recent and brand-new (!) evaluations with notes and references to earlier publications as well as general information for all those interested (including the exhibition catalogue Troia – Traum und Wirklichkeit offering a synthesis of views both old and new):

TROIA – TRAUM UND WIRKLICHKEIT, a guide to the comprehensive Trojan exhibit in Stuttgart, Braunschweig and Bonn in 2001-2002, ed. Troia Project, (Theiss-Verlag, Stuttgart 2001), in German. A Turkish version (TROIA - DÜŞ VE GERÇEK) was published in Homer Kitabevi (Istanbul 2001)

IRINA ANTONOVA, WLADIMIR TOLSTIKOV, MIKHAIL TREISTER, The Gold of Troy: Searching for Homer's Fabled City, ed. Donald Easton, catalogue of the exhibition in Moscow 1996-97 (London 1996)

BIRGIT BRANDAU, Troia, Eine Stadt und ihr Mythos: Die neuesten Entdeckungen (Berg.-Gladbach 1997)

BIRGIT BRANDAU, HARMUT SCHICKERT, PETER JABLONKA, Troia, wie es wicklich aussah (Piper TB, Munich 2004)

JOACHIM LATACZ, Troy and Homer - Towards a Solution of an Old Mystery (Oxford University Press, 2004)

MICHAEL SIEBLER, Troia: Geschichte, Grabungen, Kontroversen (Zabern, Mainz 1994)

MICHAEL SIEBLER, Troia: Mythos und Wirklichkeit (Reclam, Ditzingen 2001)

WLADIMIR P. TOLSTIKOV, MICHAIL J. TREISTER, Der Schatz aus Troja: Schliemann und der Mythos des Priamos-Goldes, a catalogue of the Moscow 1996/97 exhibition (Belser, Stuttgart/Zurich 1996)

MICHAEL WOOD, In Search of the Trojan War (London 1985)

4. Books for Young People

PETER CONNOLLY, The Legend of Odysseus, also available in German (Oxford 1986)

WALTER JENS, Ilias und Odyssee (Ravensburger, Ravensburg 1983)

THOMAS FACKLER, Troia: das Spiel, a prize-winning archaeological game (German only) for children nine years and above (Prestel, Munich 2002)

CHRISTOPH HAUSSNER, MATTIAS RAIDT, Rüya und der Traum von Troia, an illustrated novel for teenagers prepared by members of the excavation staff with a foreword by the director of excavations (Roseni, Hamm 2001)

RÜSTEM ASLAN, CHRISTOPH HAUSSNER, Troia: Neue Spuren zwischen alten Mauern, German and Turkish editions for children seven years and above (BAG, Remshalden-Grunbach 2004)

FURTHER RESOURCES:

STUDIA TROICA, dedicated to the theme "Troia and the Troad, the archaeology of a region," is the annual interdisciplinary periodical of the Troia Project. The focus of the publication is the ongoing research today. Inquiries and subscription requests may be addressed to

VERLAG PHILIPP VON ZABERN,

P.O. Box 4065

D-55030 Mainz - Germany

Tel: 089 / 12 15 16-26, * Fax: 089 / 12 15 1616

e-mail: vertrieb@zabern.de

ANNUAL VIDEO/DVD-REPORTS FROM TROİA

Annual reports of the excavation campaigns of 1988-1997are available in video with tapescripts in your choice of German, English or Turkish. More comprehensive editions were produced in 1996 (a year that marked both the 25th season of work at Troia and the 125th anniversary of the very first "dig" at the site) and in 2001 (to complement the Troia-exhibit), also available on DVD. The cooperating organization through which orders can be placed is the

INSTITUT FÜR DEN WISSENSCHAFTLICHEN FILM

Nonnenstieg 72

D-37075 Göttingen - Germany

Tel: 0551 / 50 24 160, Fax: 0551 / 50 24 400

In Gratitude

The recent excavations at Troia could never have accomplished what they have so far achieved without the participation of the many scholars who have contributed –from their homes and offices around the globe as well as in the field. Our results are a thousand and one threads of information that bind together diverse disciplines.

To these scholars as well as to the responsible Turkish officials who have assisted us –not to mention the various laborers and non-academic staff– we owe many thanks.

Included in this booklet is information from the very newest publications, including some not yet off the press. Two such examples include the chronological studies of P. Mountjoy (Athens) of the end of phase VII a (= VI i) and the investigations of the heyday of Troia/Wilusa in this period (13th century BCE) by R. Becks. Our impressions have changed greatly over time, for archaeology is a discipline very much alive; growing and changing with each new discovery, it never fails to stimulate lively discussion.

The Troia Project is most grateful to the following institutions, companies and individuals for especially generous support during the recent campaigns (1988 onwards):

The Turkish Ministry of Culture and Tourism

Dr. Süleyman Bodur, Çan (since 2002)

DaimlerChrysler AG, Stuttgart (1988-2007)

Deutsche Forschungsgemeinschaft, Bonn (since 1993)

Deutsches Archäologisches Institut, Berlin (1988-2000)

James H. Ottaway Jr., New York (since 1988)

The Institute for Aegean Prehistory, New York (since 1991)

The Institute for Mediterranean Studies, Cincinnati (since 1988)

Marianne and Dr. Hans Günter Jansen, Böblingen (since 1988)

Erdmute and Prof. Dr. Dietrich Koppenhöfer, Weinstadt (since 1988)

Mercedes-Benz Türk AŞ (since 1988)

Landesbank Baden-Württemberg, Stuttgart (2001-2002)

Siemens Sanayi ve Ticaret A.Ş (since 2002)

The Taft Semple Fund and the University of Cincinnati (since 1989)

Vereinigung der Freunde der Universität Tübingen e.V. Universitätsbund (since 1988)

Tübingen University (since 1988-2012)

Carolyn and Dr. Malcolm Wiener, New York (since 2003)

Then let us not forget the three hundred fifty or so standing members of the FRIENDS OF TROY/FREUNDE VON TROİA/TROİA DOSTLARI (Cincinnati, Tübingen and Çanakkale).

YOU, TOO, CAN BECOME A MEMBER.

LEND A HELPING HAND TO TROİA AND THE LANDSCAPE OF HOMER!

SUPPORT THE HISTORICAL NATIONAL PARK HERE!

www.troiavakfi.com

Our bank account is
Ziraat Bankası Merkez Şubesi – Çanakkale/Turkey
Troia Vakfı
Konto-Nr: 48131335-5002
IBAN: TR440001000072481313335-5002

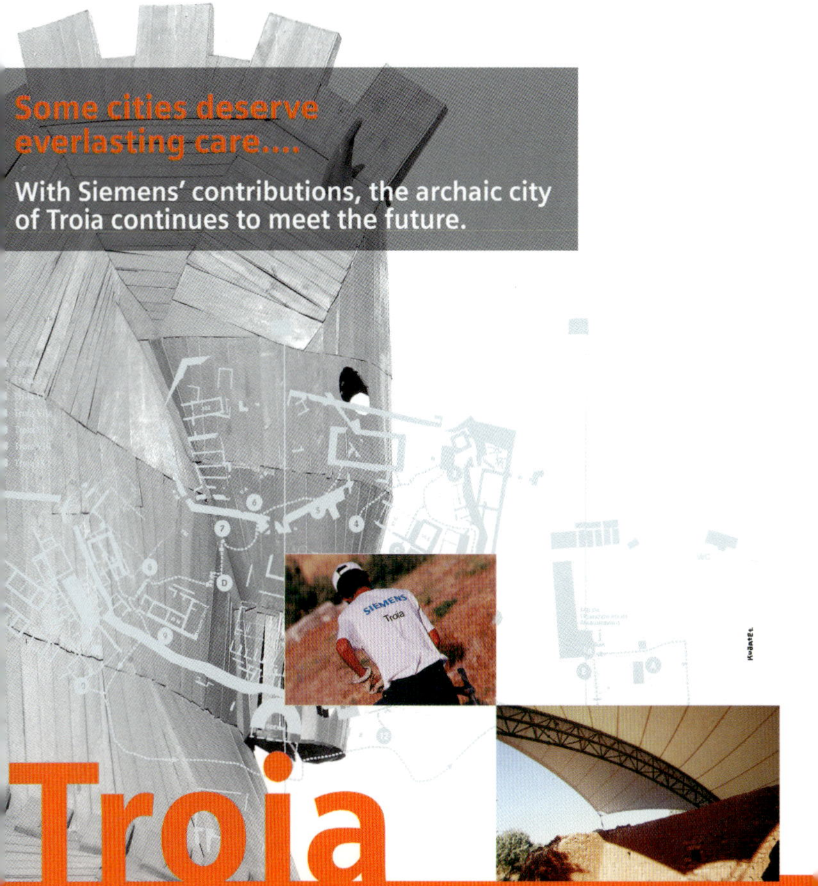

It was one of the greater necessities of our corporate social responsibility to contribute to the covering the archaic megaron structure with a roof, in order to avail it for visitors. The archaic megaron was revealed during the archeological excavations at Troia. An historical place that is included in the "Cultural Legacy" list by UNESCO, where the Anatolian and European cultures meet.

As Siemens, we are a major supporter of the efforts regarding the protection of this significant work of art from the Bronz Age, and of visually enriching the Troia archeological site.

We share the pride and satisfaction of knowing that with such contribution, light is not only shed on the past, but also on the future.

www.siemens.com.tr

SIEMENS

6
3
4
7
8
C
5
5a
D
5b
9
2
10
1b
12
11
Hamam
Bath
Bad

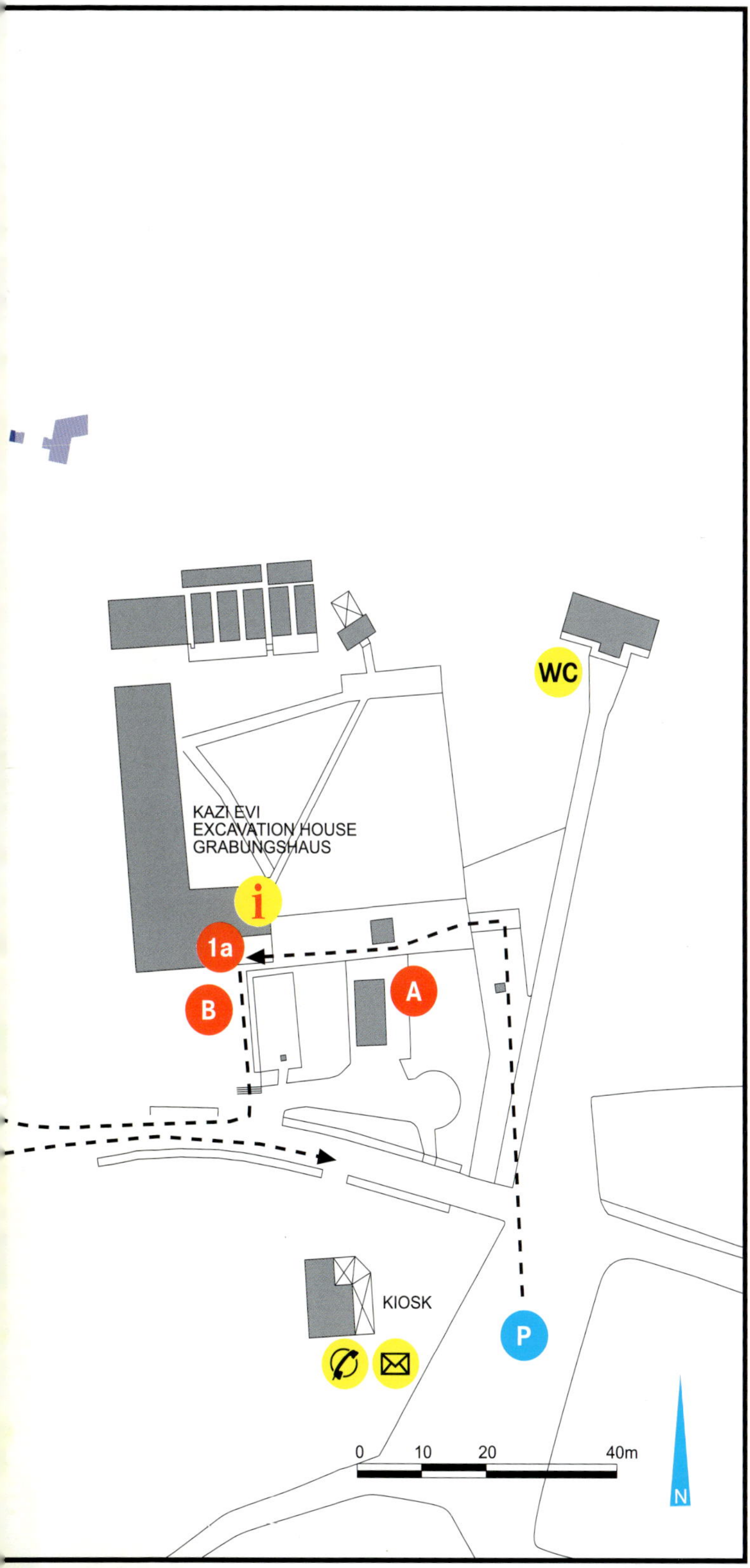

WC
KAZI EVI
EXCAVATION HOUSE
GRABUNGSHAUS
i
1a
A
B
KIOSK
P
0
10
20
40m
N

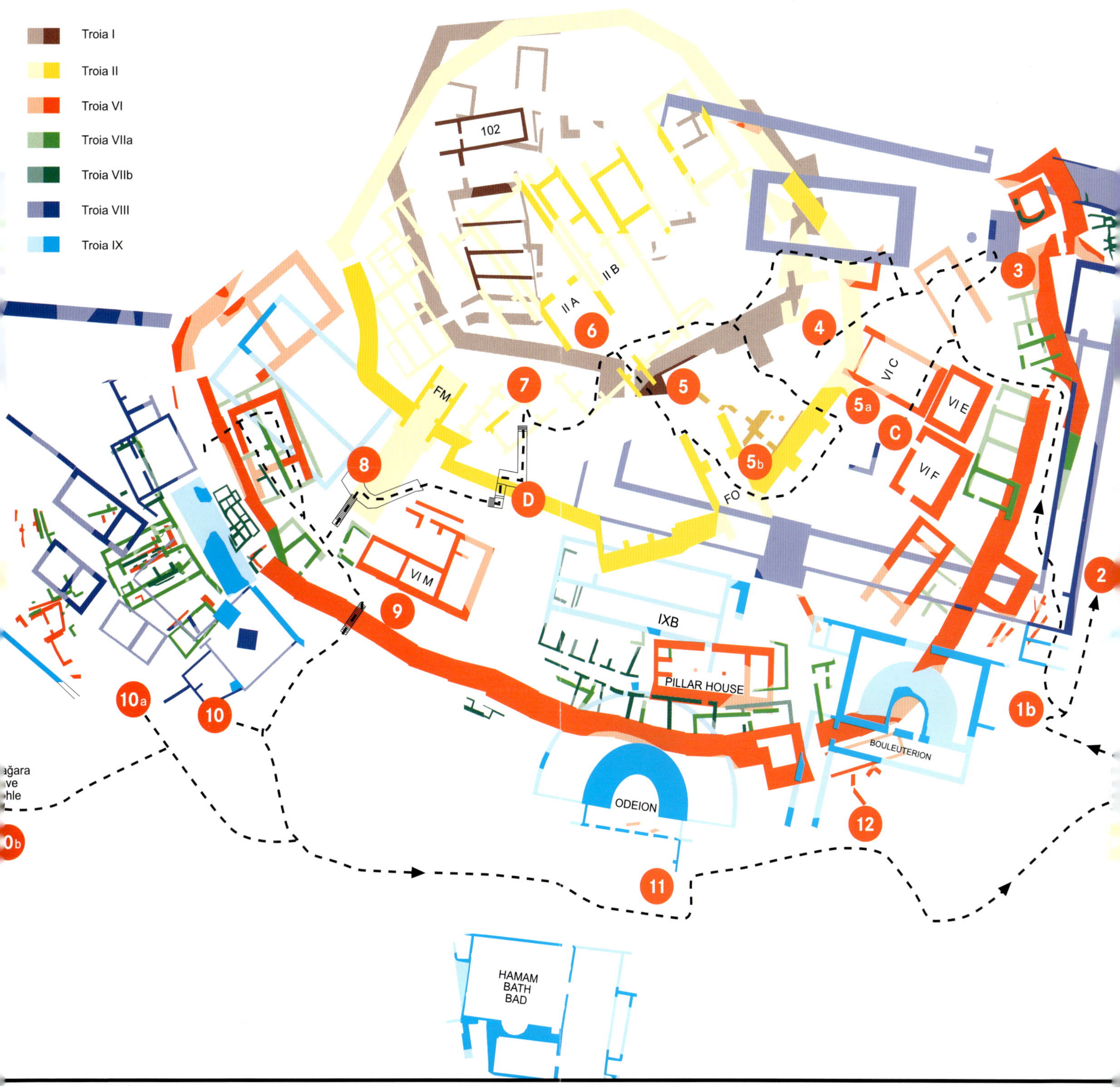
Troia I
Troia II
Troia VI
Troia VIIa
Troia VIIb
Troia VIII
Troia IX
102
II A
II B
FM
FO
VI C
VI E
VI F
VI M
IXB
PILLAR HOUSE
BOULEUTERION
ODEION
HAMAM
BATH
BAD
1b
2
3
4
5
5a
5b
6
7
8
9
10
10a
11
12
C
D